Thursday & Horn islands ○○ Cape York

Daintree Rainforest & Cape Tribulation ○

○ Port Douglas

○ Mission Beach

○ Great Barrier Reef

Boodjamulla (Lawn Hill) National Park ○

○ Magnetic Island

○ The Whitsundays

Winton ○

QUEENSLAND

Seventeen Seventy

Birdsville ○

Carnarvon National Park ○

○ Fraser Island

○ Sunshine Coast

BRISBANE ▪

Lake Eyre ○

○ Byron Bay

SOUTH AUSTRALIA

Flinders Ranges

NEW SOUTH WALES

Tamworth ○

○ Coffs Coast

Clare Valley

Mungo National Park ○

Yorke Peninsula

The Barossa ○

Blue Mountains

○ Sydney Harbour   ○ Lord Howe Island

○ Bondi Beach

ADELAIDE ▪

Murray River

Great Alpine Road

Australian War Memorial

▪ SYDNEY

○ Southern Highlands

Fleurieu Peninsula

CANBERRA ▪

○ Jervis Bay

Kangaroo Island

Daylesford

Jindabyne

○ Murramarang National Park

Grampians National Park

MCG

Yarra Valley

○ Tilba

○ Sapphire Coast

MELBOURNE ▪

Falls Creek

Great Ocean Road

Walhalla

Mount Feathertop

Great Otway National Park

Metung

Mornington Peninsula

Phillip Island

Wilsons Promontory

King Island

VICTORIA

Stanley

Bay of Fires

Cradle Mountain-Lake St Clair National Park

TASMANIA

Strahan

Bicheno

MONA

Freycinet National Park

HOBART ▪

○ Port Arthur

Bruny Island

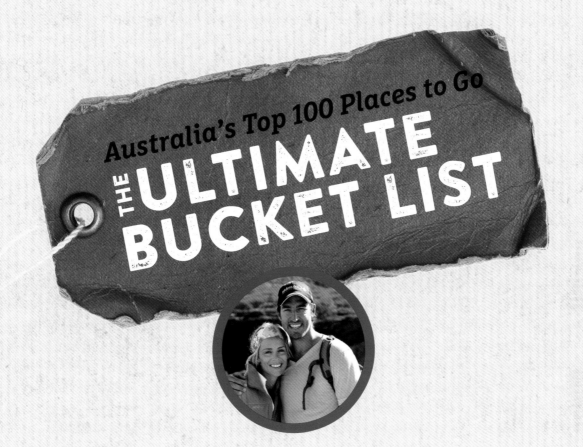

Australia's Top 100 Places to Go

THE ULTIMATE
BUCKET LIST

Australia's Top 100 Places to Go

THE ULTIMATE BUCKET LIST

Jennifer Adams & Clint Bizzell

EXPLORE
AUSTRALIA

CONTENTS

Pembroke Branch Tel. 6689575

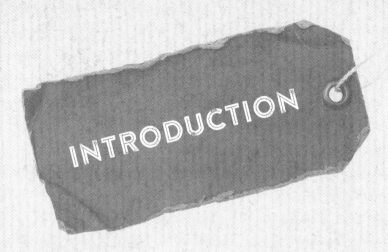

INTRODUCTION

It's not just the places we go, it's the people we meet that capture our hearts.

This book is for all the wonderful people we've met on our travels right across Australia – thank you for sharing your incredible backyards.

We've been privileged to spend the past five years travelling extensively across Australia filming for our TV travel series *Places We Go* – and what a journey it's been, not only for us and our daughter Charli, but for everyone on our team.

Putting this book together has been a wonderful and nostalgic trip for us. We've loved recounting our favourite places in Australia, almost as much as hearing from the Australian public about the places they think qualify for the *Ultimate Bucket List*. We were inundated with thousands of suggestions from all over the country, and as you'll see we've included many quotes in this book from the travellers who sent them in.

As you can imagine, it was really tough to decide which places would and wouldn't make it onto 'Australia's top 100 places to go' list; in fact it caused much debate amongst our *Places We Go* family. We know that as you flick through these pages you might not always agree with what we've chosen, but with something as subjective as this we knew it would be impossible to please everyone! Indeed, there are many more places in Australia that we love – if only we could have chosen 1000!

Our *Places We Go* crew has a tagline we always use: 'It's not just the places we go, it's the people we meet that capture our hearts.' This saying came about organically as a result of meeting such warm-hearted, wonderful locals wherever we travelled, who not only shared their love of their backyards, but also welcomed us with their warm hospitality, making our trips so memorable. To all of you, thank you.

We hope that by reading through these pages, you'll find inspiration to visit some of these wonderful places in Australia – for there are so many. We truly have a spectacular country.

Enjoy, and happy travels.

Jen and Clint

NEW SOUTH WALES & ACT

» *The eternal flame sparks reflection at the Australian War Memorial*

AUSTRALIAN WAR MEMORIAL

Standing proudly in the heart of the national capital, the Australian War Memorial immediately commands your attention and respect. Built to commemorate the sacrifice of Australians who have died in wars, it is an education, an experience and a revelation all at once.

Combining a shrine, museum and an extensive archive, the Australian War Memorial is a building for the people. Poppies adorn the bronze inscriptions on the Roll of Honour within the Commemorative Courtyard, reminding you that the fallen soldiers were more than just names; they were family members. The sheer number of names recorded here, totalling more than 102,000 soldiers, gives magnitude to this loss.

Your breath catches when you glimpse the copper Hall of Memory, housing the Tomb of the Unknown Australian Soldier. Galleries bring to life the World War I and II campaigns, cutting-edge displays share powerful stories about more recent conflicts, and a sculpture garden offers a place for quiet reflection, surrounded by memorials of our service men and women.

At the end of each day, visitors are farewelled with the Australian national anthem and the emotive sounds of the 'Last Post'. During the ceremony, one soldier's story is brought to life, a testament to the memorial that strives to ensure they are never forgotten.

Here is their spirit, in the heart of the land they loved; and here we guard the record which they themselves made.

Charles Bean (founding father of the Australian War Memorial), 1948

» *Poppies adorn the Roll of Honour*

DID YOU KNOW?

- The Australian War Memorial was opened in 1941.
- The memorial is open every day of the year except Christmas Day, and entry is free.
- The Tomb of the Unknown Australian Soldier lies within the Hall of Memory under a mosaic dome comprising over six million tiles. The unknown soldier represents all Australians who have died during wartime.

BLUE MOUNTAINS

Iconic peaks draped with a signature blue haze, the Blue Mountains are Sydney's World Heritage–listed backyard, filled with adventure, inspiration and rejuvenation.

Ten times older than the Grand Canyon, the Greater Blue Mountains region encompasses Blue Mountains National Park, 247,000 hectares of wilderness made up of sandstone ridges and peaks, tablelands, valleys, rainforests and waterfalls.

Home to more than one hundred species of eucalypts, it is the mixture of eucalyptus oil and sunlight that creates the characteristic blue haze over the mountains, setting them apart from any other range in the country. In winter, the haze blends in with smoke curling out of chimneys, and in autumn it contrasts with brilliant hues of oranges and reds as the leaves change colour.

Picturesque towns such as Katoomba, Blackheath and Leura characterise the communities of the Blue Mountains, which focus on incredible natural beauty, scenic views, colonial heritage and a vibrant food scene.

For millennia, the Gundungurra Aboriginal people have inhabited the Blue Mountains and they are still represented by the Gundungurra Tribal Council Aboriginal Corporation, based in Katoomba. In the lower Blue Mountains, the Darug people are still represented by the Darug Tribal Aboriginal Corporation. Evidence of Indigenous habitation and traditions exists in the mountains today, and includes rock art and carvings.

» *Crossing the great divide on the Scenic Skyway*

WHAT TO DO

- Explore the wilderness on one of the many bushwalks, both guided and self-guided.
- Go shopping! Boutique, antique and gourmet shopping is on offer in many of the Blue Mountains towns, and the Blackheath Growers' Market is held every second Sunday.
- Attend one of the many regular cultural events such as Oktoberfest and the Blue Mountains Music Festival, both held in Katoomba.
- Grab a picnic basket and fill it with regional goodies, then locate one of the many picnic spots in the mountains; most are blessed with panoramic views.
- Visit Scenic World for unique ways to experience the Blue Mountains, including the Scenic Skyway offering great views from 270 metres above.

The beaches surrounding Bondi are world-class and there are so many wonderful cafe and restaurant options in the area for coffee enthusiasts and foodies. When the weather is right, Bondi offers the most incredible views. Exercising around the headland is a dream come true for keen walkers and runners – such perfect scenery to sweat it out in. Bondi holidays are my favourite!

Kate Bracken, Nambour, Queensland

» *Lifeguards in action*

» *Bondi is a favourite for beachgoers*

» ***Overlooking the ocean pool at the Bondi Icebergs Club***

BONDI BEACH

One of the most famous beaches in the world, this crescent of golden sand and turquoise water, just 7 kilometres from Sydney's CBD, is perpetually buzzing with backpackers, surfers, sunbathers and stylish locals. A magnet for people who want to see and be seen, Bondi is a meeting place for everyone, and offers upmarket restaurants, boutique shopping, cafes, bars and that gorgeous, iconic beach.

Bondi is an Aboriginal word meaning 'water breaking over rocks'. The area initially became a popular attraction when it was made available to the public as a picnic ground and amusement resort between 1855 and 1877 by landowner Francis O'Brien, who originally named it O'Brien Estate. Even though O'Brien wanted to eventually restrict beach access because of its popularity, the council intervened and in 1882 Bondi became a public beach.

Though it was a working-class suburb for much of its life, today Bondi is very multicultural and is climbing towards an upper–middle-class community. The 1 kilometre stretch of sand that defines the suburb is always at the forefront of activity. From surfing, to markets, beach volleyball and many sporting and cultural events, Bondi Beach has established itself as an Australian cultural mecca.

" Even though there are so many beautiful beaches in Sydney, let alone Australia, Bondi Beach would have to be the most iconic in the country. With its postcard views and famous surf lifesavers, it's loved the world over.

As soon as we arrive in Sydney, the first thing we love to do is take a morning run along the spectacular coastline between Bondi and Bronte, followed by a dip in the ocean and a morning latte at one of the many cool cafes in the side streets. Sometimes we just sit for hours and watch the locals and travellers who contribute to the irresistible, relaxed Bondi vibe of surfing and happy days.

We have spent many afternoons at Bondi Icebergs Club. With the waves crashing up against this ocean pool, you can feel its long history and follow in the footsteps of all the avid swimmers who have been using the pool since 1929. There's nothing better than the feeling of a swim in winter when the water is crisp and the sky is blue – talk about invigorating!

A big hello to the wonderful surf lifesavers who patrol our beaches! "

JEN AND CLINT

PLACES WE GO

DID YOU KNOW?

- Bondi Beach was added to the Australian National Heritage List in 2008.
- Between 1935 and 1961 the Local Government Act, Ordinance No. 52, governed the decency of swimming costumes, resulting in public controversy. Council inspectors would measure dimensions of swimwear and order offenders off the beach. The most famous example of this was when Hollywood actress Jean Parker was escorted from the beach in 1951 because her bikini was deemed too skimpy.
- Pods of whales and dolphins can be sighted in the bay around Bondi during annual migration periods.
- Founded in 1907, Bondi Surf Bathers' Life Saving Club is claimed to be the first surf lifesaving club in the world.

BYRON BAY

Known the world over for its relaxed lifestyle, expansive beaches, alternative philosophies and natural wonders, Byron Bay, a laid-back but chic town on the northern coast of New South Wales, is synonymous with 'the good life'.

This is a place where it's easy to indulge, and having a good time is what it's all about. Byron's surf culture, with a touch of hedonism, has been drawing visitors to its shores for decades. It's a haven for adventurers, offering surfing, fishing, whale-watching and hang-gliding, amongst other activities, and is also a magnet for the artistic and alternative, its splendid raw beauty providing inspiration for a natural and creative lifestyle.

While Byron's scenery boasts a breathtaking hinterland as its backdrop and a stunning coastline dotted with dramatic headlands as its main event, Byron Bay is also known for its welcoming and proud locals, and entertainment aplenty. Many city dwellers have escaped here for a more relaxed environment with adventure in their backyard. They are the first in Australia to glimpse the sunrise, and probably some of the last to crawl into bed at night.

But during the day, locals and visitors alike enjoy the lifestyle that casts a spell over everyone who passes through, making it almost impossible not to return.

" Byron Bay is known for its healing qualities; indeed, the locals always seem to have that 'Byron glow'. We have to admit that whenever we visit we feel somewhat recalibrated afterwards, thanks to its beautiful beaches and lush hinterland. There's nothing better than when we grab a surfboard and join locals and tourists alike for our first surf here each time we visit.

While it's been developed over the years, it's kept its hippy vibe of yesteryear, and is always filled with travellers from all over the world. Surfing, yoga, lots of fresh organic food, great pubs and an awesome live-music scene have contributed to many wonderful memories for us over the years.

One of our most treasured memories was experiencing the Byron Bay Bluesfest, a world-music festival that attracts incredible artists from across the globe. It's packed with people dressing up in all manner of costumes, all there for a good time enjoying the Byron magic. I'll never forget spending the afternoon with Aussie country music legend Troy Cassar-Daley. He came to our campsite with his guitar and, as you can imagine, drew quite a crowd. "

JEN AND CLINT

PLACES WE GO

WHAT TO DO

- Visit one of Byron's markets, from community markets to farmers markets and artisan markets, there's something for everyone.

- Catch a gig at any of the live-music venues in town. Barely a night passes where live entertainment is not scheduled, showcasing local, national and international talent.

- Join the locals seeking a more balanced body and mind at any one of the yoga retreats in and out of town.

- Get involved in what Byron does best: watersports galore! From surfing and fishing to kayaking, paddleboarding and more, it's a must to get out there and take advantage of the beaches.

- Visit Cape Byron, a headland that forms part of the world's oldest caldera (the rim of an enormous extinct volcano). Here you'll find the Cape Byron Lighthouse, completed in 1901, and a breathtaking view that sometimes includes pods of dolphins and humpback whales.

» The sun always shines in Byron

The bohemian beachside town of Byron Bay has the key to my heart (and my inner hippy!). It's a complete melting pot of both ends of the social scale, from the uber-rich to 1970s flashbacks living off the grid, but it works. The sound of buskers on street corners, the smell of vegan curries and shopping in designer-gypsy fashion stores all lift my spirit. Not to mention the whales, the lighthouse walk, the beautiful hinterland, the surf ... I simply *love* Byron Bay!

**Lauren Gunthorpe,
Sunshine Beach, Queensland**

» *Cape Byron Lighthouse, Australia's most easterly point*

» *Surfing is a way of life in Byron*

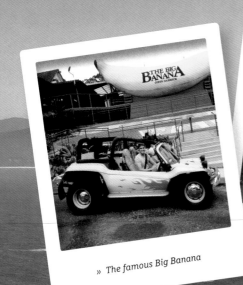

» The famous Big Banana

» A family-friendly destination

» *A house with a view on South Solitary Island*

COFFS COAST

A magical stretch of coastline in the north of New South Wales where you can do as much or as little as you like, Coffs Coast is one of the country's best family holiday destinations. With the town of Coffs Harbour at its heart, the region is said to have the most liveable climate in Australia. Nestled as it is between a mountain range and dozens of beautiful beaches, fresh mountain and ocean air is always around you, and subtropical waters await.

Once a major banana plantation area, it might be quirkily famous for its Big Banana landmark, but these days the region is equally invested in blueberries, tourism and fishing.

With 90 kilometres of coastline running alongside a tapestry of national parks, mountain escarpments, seaside villages and hinterland communities, Coffs Coast has something for everyone. You can camp at beautiful Nambucca Heads or visit Australia's largest regional markets in Bellingen. You'll find excellent fishing in Macksville, and a nature lover's paradise in Dorrigo National Park with its waterfalls, wildlife and walking tracks. In Coffs Harbour itself, dozens of beaches are home to a plethora of accommodation, and the Jetty Strip, with its many restaurants, is one of the most popular attractions for both locals and tourists.

National parks are just a short drive away, with an amazing network of walking trails from which you can look out over incredible panoramic vistas. Coffs Coast is also one of the best spots to witness the annual humpback whale migration from May until November.

» *Scenery offshore*

WHAT TO DO

- Discover the Coffs Coast waterways by canoe, kayak or stand-up paddleboard.
- Join a fishing charter or learn how to sail on the many boats available.
- Go whitewater rafting on the Nymboida River in the Coffs hinterland.
- Dive or snorkel the subtropical waters of the Solitary Islands Marine Reserve.
- Hop on your bicycle and explore the 18 cycling routes along Coffs Coast.

JERVIS BAY

Known for its white sand, marine park and coastal wilderness, Jervis Bay, a sheltered inlet of the Pacific Ocean, ticks all the boxes for an unspoiled paradise.

One of only two marine parks in New South Wales, and also a national park, the area stands out for its significant natural beauty. People are drawn to its clear waters and its beaches (which are considered to be some of the best in the country), and wildlife abounds. Seals and dolphins call the bay home, and whales on their north- and south-bound migrations pass by the entrance to the inlet. For this reason, Jervis Bay is one of the best whale-watching destinations in the country, especially because the whales can be seen from land as well as the sea.

The bay's seaside villages (including the main town of Huskisson), markets, coastal forests and wineries offer other good reasons to visit. Walking tracks lead through some of the most spectacular coastal scenery in the country, and the White Sands walk to Hyams Beach will take you to the whitest sand in the world, according to Guinness World Records.

Walk, swim, kayak, cruise, dive or fish: Jervis Bay is a true year-round adventure playground in one of the most beautiful settings imaginable.

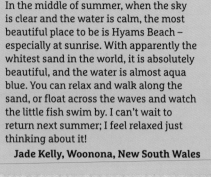

" We absolutely loved Jervis Bay. Everything is centred on the water, which is beautifully framed by the surrounding national park. The whole region has a simplicity about it and the bay evokes a wonderful calm.

Before visiting Hyams Beach, we wondered about the Guinness World Records claim that it had the whitest sand in the world, thinking 'really, how white can white be?'. But as soon as we stepped onto the silky smooth sand, we agreed that it's definitely up there with the whitest sand we've ever seen – it's so white, it's almost blinding! The rolling, aqua-coloured waves of the Pacific Ocean contrasted beautifully with the sand, and in no time we were bodysurfing in the crystal-clear water.

There must be something special in the water here, as a boat ride we took out to the marine park attested. Some 80 to 120 bottlenose dolphins reside here and a pod came straight up to our boat and started playing with us – one of the dolphins kept rolling on its back looking straight up at us, obviously loving the attention. Apparently experiences like this are a common occurrence in the bay; indeed, the following morning we were out paddleboarding and we could see dolphins playing in the water just metres away. "

JEN AND CLINT

PLACES WE GO ▶

WHAT TO DO

- Board a whale-watching cruise to see humpbacks and an occasional southern right whale on their yearly migration. On the way, spot some of the wild bottlenose dolphins who live here year-round.
- Try sea-kayaking on the protected waters of the marine park.
- Scuba dive at one of the most diverse diving spots along Australia's east coast.
- Visit Booderee National Park, formerly Jervis Bay National Park, home to spectacular beaches and bushwalks.

» Surf's up (or not) while
paddleboarding

» Charli gazing out at
dolphins in the bay

» Kayaking over the man-made lake

» A moody Lake Jindabyne

» *These wild brumbies haven't yet encountered the* Man from Snowy River

JINDABYNE

The shores of beautiful Lake Jindabyne are home to the town of Jindabyne, gateway to the alpine paradise of Kosciuszko National Park in the Snowy Mountains. The poem, *The Man from Snowy River*, was inspired by the region's mountain horsemen, and the area still evokes the sense of adventure immortalised in Banjo Paterson's famous words.

Everywhere you look, the surrounding mountains and bushland frame the lake, and life seems to revolve around it for locals and visitors. People sit by the edge of the water and fish, content to wait for their catch, while the more active tackle the surrounding landscape on mountain bikes. There's a plethora of bushwalks available too, meandering between the forest and the water.

On the lake itself, a favourite pastime is kayaking or canoeing, paddling over what was the original town of Jindabyne, which was flooded and relocated in the 1960s to make way for the Snowy Mountains Hydro-Electric Scheme.

You can ski at the alpine resorts of Thredbo and Perisher, which are just a short drive away, or horseride with wild brumbies on a breathtaking sanctuary in the foothills. Whatever you do, drink in the views and the fresh mountain air; it's a sure-fire way to add a bit of spark to your spirit.

" It really is quite incredible to think that the town of Jindabyne was moved for one of Australia's greatest engineering feats, and remnants of it actually remain in the lake today. You'd never know, though. On the day we arrived, we joined the hype of activity on the lake in kayaks, surrounded by stunning snow-capped mountains. Later, we set up camp right beside Lake Jindabyne. It was autumn at the time, and the trees were alight with the most vibrantly coloured leaves – it was a truly glorious setting.

After reciting Banjo Paterson's famous poem, *The Man from Snowy River*, we were inspired to get into the hills on horseback for an afternoon that turned out to be quite magical. We joined Justin from Snowy Wilderness, which not only offers horserides that can last a few hours, a day or a week, but also provides a sanctuary for the beloved brumby.

The views were breathtaking: we could see Australia's highest peak, Mount Kosciuszko, and Mount Perisher in the background. But nothing compared to coming up over a hill and seeing a mob of brumbies galloping like the wind, then gathering together and basking in the afternoon sun. It was the perfect Snowy Mountains experience. "

JEN AND CLINT

PLACES WE GO

DID YOU KNOW?

- When the lake's water levels are low, parts of the submerged original town can be seen above the water.
- One hundred thousand men from 30 different countries worked for 25 years on the Snowy Mountains Hydro-Electric Scheme. It is the largest engineering project that's ever been carried out in Australia.
- Rainbow trout were released into the lake in 1894, beginning a fishing tradition that continues to this day.

LORD HOWE ISLAND

» The last paradise

Known as the 'last paradise', Lord Howe Island, 660 kilometres off the New South Wales coast, is said to be the most beautiful island in the Pacific. If you visit, you'll be one of only 400 guests allowed on the island at any one time in order to protect the pristine environment and unhurried lifestyle.

You get around on bike or foot on Lord Howe. There are no cars, and the priority is to relax and enjoy the abundance of activities and adventures that nature has to offer.

Hiking one of the island's peaks, Mount Gower, is one of the world's great walks. Down at sea level, fishing, surfing, sailing and scuba diving allow you to take advantage of the incredible marine environment with crystal-clear waters, coral reefs which are among the best in the world, and over 60 dive sites.

Handfeed multiple species of fish by simply stepping off the sand at Neds Beach. Or have superb North Bay beach all to yourself, with nothing other than migratory seabirds, turtles and a historic shipwreck for company.

World Heritage listed, the island is nature at its finest. And best of all, its remote location and strict sustainability measures ensure it will stay that way. And best of all, its remote location and strict sustainability measures ensure it will stay that way.

An amazingly beautiful place, Lord Howe Island is full of stunning beaches, great walking tracks and an abundance of wildlife. The weather is mild, the water is warm and the island is small enough to cycle around in a day, yet big enough to be away from it all. I cannot think of a better place to go to relax, unwind and enjoy Australian nature at its best!

**Carolyn Stephenson,
Surrey Hills, Victoria**

Complete paradise. Go rainforest walking barefoot. Swim in crystal-clear lagoon waters. Go surfing. Cycle or walk around the island – there's no need for a car. There's beautiful wildlife, including turtles, woodhens and many seabirds, and awesome fishing, especially for tuna and kingfish. Barbecue your fish at a public beach or eat it as sashimi. Lord Howe has a special place in my heart; once you go there, no other destination compares.

**Angela Head, Clarence Town,
New South Wales**

WHAT TO DO

- Go catch a fish! With no commercial fishing and an environment surrounded by marine park, Lord Howe Island is legendary as a fishing destination.
- Snorkel some of the best coral reefs in the world, just metres from the shore, or visit one of the many dive sites for a deeper underwater experience.
- Take your pick from a range of accommodation, from lodges to luxury houses, knowing it will never be crowded on Lord Howe.

» *The eroded 'Walls of China' sand sculptures*

MUNGO NATIONAL PARK

» *The eerily beautiful landscape*

With ancient fossilised lake beds, dune fields, sand plains and lunettes (half-moon-shaped sand dunes), Mungo National Park could pass for a landscape on another planet. Stretching out beneath an enormous outback sky in New South Wales' Willandra Lakes World Heritage area, it is not only the arid environment that makes this area so unique, but also its history, which is almost unmatched in significance by any other Australian destination.

It is here that the earliest evidence of human existence outside Africa was discovered. 'Mungo Lady' and 'Mungo Man' are the oldest human remains to be found in Australia, dating back 42,000 years. Evidence also shows that Aboriginal people were living at Mungo for at least 45,000 years, surviving the last Ice Age. Footprints of the Willandra people, dating back 20,000 years, were discovered in 2003 and historic artefacts preserved in the ideal conditions of the park represent a lineage that extends over two thousand generations.

It is this history combined with the inimitable beauty of the environment that sets the park apart. Only designated a national park in 1979 when its land, which was used for cattle grazing between 1860 and 1978, was sold back to the National Parks and Wildlife Service, Mungo now preserves both its precious Indigenous and pastoral histories for visitors to discover.

Mungo National Park is a stunning outback spot full of archaeological wonder and awe-inspiring history set amongst a spectacular lunar landscape. Drive through the expansive dry lakes and explore the Walls of China at dawn or dusk when the colours are most breathtaking. Tour with an Aboriginal ranger, camp under the stars and experience the magic and wonder that is Mungo.

Miriam Blaker, Hurstbridge, Victoria

WHAT TO DO

- Join representatives of the Paakantji, Ngyiampaa and Mutthi Mutthi tribal groups to follow in the footsteps of their ancestors on an Aboriginal discovery tour.
- Stroll along the 'Walls of China' boardwalk, which offers dramatic views of the Lake Mungo lunette, shaped by erosion into sculpted sand and clay formations.
- Visit the original Mungo woolshed where, at one time, 50,000 sheep were shorn per season.

MURRAMARANG NATIONAL PARK

A scenic four-hour drive from Sydney will bring you to Murramarang National Park. Bush literally meets the ocean on this dramatic coastline, with pristine beaches so beautiful, kangaroos can't resist bounding along the secluded stretches of sand. Explore the rugged headlands, enjoy the plentiful fishing spots and complete your blissful days camping around a fire. The friendliness of the small, local communities adds to the laid-back holiday vibe.

Vanessa Croan, Sydney, New South Wales

One of New South Wales' best-kept secrets, Murramarang National Park, stretches 44 kilometres along the South Coast and is like walking into a timeless land. Here undisturbed coastline meets spotted gum forest, dramatic headlands house hidden sea caves, and wallabies graze freely as the sun goes down.

Aboriginal people have lived in this area for thousands of years, and their rich culture and heritage can be easily discovered throughout the 11,977-hectare park, with shell middens and tool manufacturing sites still evident.

This is a place that's been virtually unchanged by humans, and offers an unspoilt experience amongst some of the state's best natural environments. The beaches offer surfing, secluded swimming spots and birdwatching opportunities, while the undisturbed bush is great for spotting wildlife. It's also not uncommon to see eastern grey kangaroos lounging near the beach or your campsite!

If you're not surfing the waves or walking along remote beaches, venture along one of the many walking trails in the park to discover verdant rainforest, Durras Lake, incredible rock formations rising from the sea or million-dollar views from Durras Mountain.

» *Driving through verdant rainforest*

WHAT TO DO

- Walk around Durras Lake, particularly if you like birdwatching; nectar-seeking honeyeaters, parrots and finches are common here.
- Climb from Pretty Beach to the top of Durras Mountain for incredible views.
- Go fishing off the rocks, the beach or in the lake.

» Wallabies graze freely

» *Some of the coast's famous whales have a sense of show!*

SAPPHIRE COAST

The charm of the Sapphire Coast is its dazzling beaches. Interspersed with national parks, lakes, cliffs, caves, seaside towns and scenic drives, it is the southernmost coastal region in New South Wales and a haven for holidaymakers.

Stretching from Bermagui in the north to the Victorian border in the south, the main towns of the Sapphire Coast include Bega, Tathra, Merimbula, Eden and Pambula, each offering something a little unique and all within an easy drive of each other.

Legendary for its seafood, oysters are a particularly popular export from the region, and visitors don't have to look far to get them, as most towns have their own harvest of Sydney rock oysters. The only problem is deciding which town does them best.

Whales are regular visitors here, and have been associated with the coast and particularly the waters around Eden since the early 19th century when whaling was its major industry. Today it is all about watching these gentle giants, and whether it's from the shore or by boat every experience is thrilling.

The dairy industry around Bega is famous, and cheese is still its number-one industry, although tourism is quickly catching up.

Ben Boyd National Park, named after a 19th-century entrepreneur, is a significant area for the local Yuin people. It's known for its rugged, red coastline, pristine beaches, coastal heath and Boyd's Tower, which marks the entrance to Twofold Bay and was used back in the day as a whale lookout.

» It's called Eden for a reason

» Bournda Beach at sunrise

WHAT TO DO

- Take the Merimbula boardwalk, a lovely 3.4-kilometre journey with scenic views and informative signs along the way indicating the local marine and plant life
- Try Bega's famous cheese at the Bega Cheese Heritage Centre, which provides information about the history of the dairy industry in the region
- Join a whale-watching tour from Eden or Merimbula. The Sapphire Coast is one of the few places in the world where you can see whales feeding during migration

SOUTHERN HIGHLANDS

The Southern Highlands is a unique area that makes visitors feel like they are entering another world. Apart from drawcards such as magnificent gardens, antiques, wondrous natural and heritage attractions, it's a place to relax, escape, unwind and rejuvenate within easy reach of two of Australia's major cities. It's where my heart longs to be.

Helen Schulz, East Maitland, New South Wales

Rolling green hills meet charming, old-world villages, Georgian buildings house antique stores and galleries, and cellar doors welcome visitors like old friends. The Southern Highlands is a sophisticated escape from the city, offering relaxation and indulgence with genuine country hospitality.

The 'Highlands' sit between 500m and 900m above sea level on the Great Dividing Range, and activity largely centres around the towns of Mittagong, Bowral, Moss Vale, Berrima, Bundanoon and Robertson. Some villages are famous for their historic architecture, grand gardens and food and wine, while others are the gateway to natural treasures, including national parks and some of the region's spectacular waterfalls, including Fitzroy Falls.

Once occupied by the Dhawawal Aboriginal people, the first European explorers came through in 1798 and settlement in the region occured around 1820. In 1830 the town of Berrima was planned and developed as the centre of the Highlands, but it was superseded by other nearby towns soon after. Today, however, it remains the last intact Georgian-period town on mainland Australia. The rest of the region is known for its heritage streetscapes and Georgian manors, which today house sophisticated accommodation for visitors.

The area has grown as a small but not insignificant cellar door region, the temperate climate making it a good place for chardonnay, riesling, sauvignon blanc, pinot noir and cabernet sauvignon.

» *The Tulip Time Festival in full bloom*

WHAT TO DO

- Visit Morton National Park, home to Fitzroy Falls; a spectacular waterfall cascading over a sandstone plateau and through thick green eucalypt forest to the valley below.
- Drop by Kangaroo Valley, a National Trust–listed village offering streets filled with cafes, galleries, pubs and bush cabins.
- Come in spring for the Tulip Time Festival in Bowral's Corbett Gardens, an annual event that dates back to 1911.
- If you are a cricket fan, visit the International Cricket Hall of Fame and Bradman Oval in Bowral.

» *The bridge has become the symbol of Sydney Harbour*

SYDNEY HARBOUR

» Sydney Opera House's iconic white sails

» Kayaking on the harbour

It's one of the most famous sights in the world: the Sydney Opera House's famous white sails on the edge of the harbour with the distinctive Sydney Harbour Bridge in the background and a Manly ferry thrown in for good measure. Iconic the view may be, but there is way more to this precinct than just its spectacular vista. Dig a little beneath the surface and you'll discover other reasons for why this area of Australia's largest city is such a drawcard.

Sydney's incredible history starts in the Rocks. Located directly harbour-side beneath the bridge, this was the first location where European settlers stepped ashore in Australia and is now a magnificent blend of old and new.

Positioned on an inlet called Sydney Cove, neighbouring Circular Quay, is the hub of the harbour. It hosts most attractions taking place around the area and is always buzzing with activity. Ferries come and go, restaurants, cafes and boutique shops attract locals and tourists alike, and the Opera House and botanical gardens are accessed via a walkway.

On any given night of the year, the harbour plays host to one of Sydney's great events or festivals. World-famous names grace stages inside and outside the Opera House, and the city comes here to eat, play, celebrate and marvel, often all at the same time.

On the water, the harbour is always alive with yachts, ferries and kayaks. Paddle, sail or cruise around the inlets and bays and glimpse lavish harbour-side homes and other iconic attractions such as Luna Park and Taronga Zoo.

One of my greatest memories is looking across Sydney Harbour at night during the 2000 Olympics to the famous five rings shining brightly on the bridge. I've never swum in the harbour, but I've sailed, caught the Manly ferry and paddled on her waters. Just as brilliant is running around the Opera House to Mrs Macquaries Chair or taking one of the many walks that meander around the area. Do any of these activities at sunrise or sunset and you'll be in heaven.

Tiffany Cherry, Albert Park, Victoria

WHAT TO DO

- Catch a ferry to Cockatoo Island, a heritage-listed convict site in the middle of the harbour, and camp overnight completely surrounded by the lights of Sydney.
- Get above the crowds by climbing the Sydney Harbour Bridge and enjoying a 360-degree view.
- See the city icons onboard a ferry from Circular Quay to Manly.

TAMWORTH

I'm a city girl with a little bit of country in me ... but then again, aren't we all?

The Tamworth Country Music Festival is the perfect dose of country, and probably the friendliest event on earth! The heat, the dust, the cowboys, the cowgirls, the hay, the rodeos, the buskers, it's all here ... and everyone's here to have a good time. Accommodation is pretty much booked out from year to year, so opting for a homestay is a good idea. Leave the city behind, don your hat and boots, and come play ... It's definitely worth the trek.

Liz Dayney-Morrissey, Paddington, New South Wales

Every January, country music aficionados descend on the regional New South Wales city of Tamworth to celebrate Australian country music at one of the world's biggest music festivals. Established names play the big stages and buskers line Peel Street, the main street of town, which becomes pedestrian-only during the event. The 'Golden Guitar' awards are the climax of the ten-day party, which has been running since 1973 and has hosted people like Kenny Rogers, Troy Cassar-Daley, Kasey Chambers and Keith Urban who credits the festival as being the launching pad for his career.

Visitors bring their whole family, and accommodation books out months in advance. The atmosphere is that of a big, fun, friendly street party with music performed in around 120 venues plus side events. Be treated to the entire spectrum from classic country, bluegrass, country rock, folk, blues, world music, bush ballads and line dancing. The atmosphere, camaraderie and music ensure that even visitors who are not country-music lovers will leave converted.

If you can't make it for the festival, Tamworth is still worth a visit to experience its love of country music in other forms, such as the 12-metre-high Big Golden Guitar, one of Australia's many 'big' structures, and the Hands of Fame, handprints of country music luminaries. And it's not even always about twanging guitars; this is horse country too, with various equine-related events filling out the festival calendar and plenty of places to go trail riding.

DID YOU KNOW?

- Over 2500 events are staged in 120 venues, and over 800 artists perform during the Tamworth country music festival.
- Joy McKean received the first ever Golden Guitar award in 1973 for her song 'Lights on the Hill', made popular by her husband Slim Dusty.
- The number of visitors to the festival (50,000) effectively doubles the town's population each year.
- Tent cities are erected throughout the town and region to cope with the accommodation demand during the festival.

» Fun street-party atmosphere

The Two Story
BED & BREAKFAST
Enquire in Shop..

KLEER · KUBE · PARTY
ICE
SOLD HERE

Fax Centre

Pay it at Post
Bill Payment Service

WARNING
Ph: 133 277

» Charming historic shops in town

» The rolling hills of grass are greener in Tilba

» Interrupting Jen enjoying a slice of fudge

TILBA

A short drive inland from New South Wales' south coast, the Tilba region is a glimpse into the past where two heritage villages, Central Tilba and Tilba Tilba, perfectly preserve their farming culture, turn-of-the-century architecture and pristine natural beauty.

Settled mostly during the gold-rush years of the 1890s and 1900s, the villages' combined populations today total only around 100. Residents are made up of farmers and artisans of all forms – including leather-makers, woodturners and jewellers – who have set up their businesses in the original village buildings.

This is a region where community is king, and visitors are welcomed like old friends. Local cheeses are made at the historic ABC Cheese Factory, established in 1891, using milk straight from a local farm's jersey cows. Visit the old sweet shop or Mrs Jamieson's Tilba Fudge shop and enjoy bantering with the locals. You can also drive through the rolling green hills, dotted with livestock and dominated by majestic Mount Gulaga, to see why people love living here so much.

The mountain is just one site in the region that is of spiritual significance to the local Yuin Aboriginal people. Gulaga National Park was handed back to the Aboriginal communities in 2006, and is described as being the place of ancestral origin for all Yuin people, with the mountain itself representing the mother.

Nothing will warm you to this place more than a community event, such as the Tilba Growers Market or the annual Easter festival, where the passion of the locals ignites as they all come together to celebrate this fine region they call home.

> "It's not often you find a place where beautiful green farmland hills roll all the way to the ocean, but that's how it is on the South Coast of New South Wales. This area is home to many treasures, and historic Tilba is certainly one of them. Driving there through the lush hills filled with jersey cows and old farmhouses, it feels like you've stepped into a scene out of *All Creatures Great and Small*.
>
> Settled during the gold rush, the town centre of Central Tilba is teeming with character and charm, and overflowing with art-and-craft shops. Passionate producers stock the local cafes with scrumptious, locally produced food. We tasted some of Mrs Jamieson's Tilba Fudge – homemade, of course – although we didn't get through all of the 100-plus varieties!
>
> We spent an afternoon at the historic ABC Cheese Factory, which was established as the first cheese cooperative in New South Wales. Now the home of South Coast Cheese, it is owned and run by Erica and Nic Dibden, who live on their farm nearby (with their 500 milking cows). We were lucky enough to be invited to their property. When we turned up, Nic was tending to the vegetable patch and Erica introduced us to her 'girls', the jersey cows, saying: 'Tilba's beauty is never lost on us. I spend many an afternoon looking out over the rolling hills thinking how lucky I am.'"

JEN AND CLINT

PLACES WE GO

WHAT TO DO

- Attend one of the tastings or cheese-making courses run by South Coast Cheese, which produces speciality local products in the old ABC Cheese Factory.

- Visit Foxglove Gardens, which represent the love, care and pride the local people feel for their region, being 3.5 magnificent acres of resplendent gardens that have been planted to match the seasons for around 30 years.

- Simply take a walk through the historical villages to discover local produce, meet the locals and soak up the atmosphere of yesteryear.

VICTORIA

Daylesford has it all: delicious food, beautiful scenery, spas galore. Every time we come here we feel a world away from everyday life and are so relaxed. You're sure to find a bargain or two at many of the wonderful shops in this great country town with friendly locals. And, of course, there's the Lake House, which has been featured many times on *Masterchef*!

Chris Sharman, Derrimut, Victoria

» *Full of country lanes to meander down*

» *The iconic Lake House and its famous restaurant are always worth a visit*

DAYLESFORD

» Daylesford's lake

Tucked away in the foothills of the Great Dividing Range, about 1.5-hour's drive from Melbourne, is one of Victoria's treasures. A picturesque town that offers indulgence and relaxation, Daylesford was originally settled as a goldmining town in the 1850s, but when natural mineral springs were found in the area, they soon took over as the main attraction.

Today the springs are still one of the town's biggest drawcards, and Daylesford is a popular escape for city dwellers or people just looking for that perfect country town in which to unwind. Blessed with over 70 natural mineral springs with therapeutic and healing properties, there is a plethora of wellness retreats, healing centres and spas available for pampering.

But there are also plenty of other reasons to visit. The village itself is full of boutique shopping, cafes, beautiful gardens, galleries, bookshops, antique stores and delicatessens. One of its iconic landmarks is the Convent Gallery. Originally built in the gold-rush era as a private mansion, it was bought by the Catholic Church and converted into the Holy Cross Convent and Boarding School for Girls in the 1880s, and remained so until 1973. Today it has been restored and is a resplendent venue offering a cafe, restaurant, retail space and renowned art gallery.

" On any given trip to Daylesford, you can always be assured of some R&R. It's got 'quiet country getaway' written all over it, with its day spas, lavender farms and incredible restaurants. Driving through pretty Wombat State Forest to get there starts the process of peeling away the stress of city life. By the time you arrive in town, you're all prepped to soak in the thermal springs!

Whether it's been a weekend away with friends, or some time out together, we've always found ourselves enjoying a slower pace of life here. From a crackling fire with a good glass of red in the middle of winter to a long lazy breakfast followed by a visit to one of the many day spas, it's easy to just be in the moment.

The locals in Daylesford all seem to have a connection with food and the environment, so it's no surprise that the food here is deliciously good for the soul. On one visit, we enjoyed fine dining at the iconic Lake House, where we also stayed the night and relished waking up in the morning to the sound of kookaburras and the tranquillity of the lake.

Daylesford is definitely a place where time seems to slow down. Even so, before you know it, your weekend is over and you're back in the car heading towards the city ... dreaming of next time. "

JEN AND CLINT

PLACES WE GO ▶

WHAT TO DO

- Don't miss the Lake House restaurant on Lake Daylesford, especially if you're a foodie. Part of the Lake House accommodation complex, the hatted restaurant is renowned nationally as the gourmet heart of the region.
- Visit any one of the spas or retreats around Daylesford or neighbouring Hepburn Springs for some rejuvenation.
- Enjoy Lake Daylesford on the Peace Mile walk around its perimeter, or hire a paddleboat to admire the view from the water.

FALLS CREEK

When the temperatures drop and the snow begins to fall in the south-east of Australia, skiers and snowboarders flock to the Alps and Falls Creek becomes a buzzing winter playground. In Victoria's High Country, the alpine village of Falls Creek is actually an incredible year-round destination thanks to its location within the beautiful Alpine National Park, but the winter wonderland it transforms into for around four months of the year is not to be missed.

With the state's steepest trails and a village full of ski lodges, pubs, cafes and shops, the resort can accommodate around 4500 people each night, and more as daytrippers. Everyone comes together to create a lively après-ski atmosphere when the lifts close for the day. With the ski village tucked into the same area as the chairlift, everything can be accessed on skis.

Falls Creek's first lodge was built in 1948 by workers from the Kiewa Hydro-Electric Scheme in the nearby Kiewa Valley, and the first chairlift in Australia was built here in 1957. Since then, the mountain has hosted winter revellers every year who traverse its 1110 acres of ski fields with 92 runs, all looking out over the spectacular Victorian High Country and beautiful Mount Bogong.

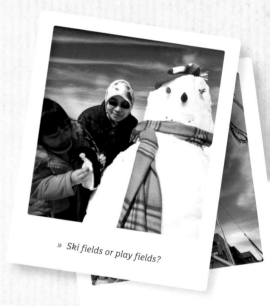

» Ski fields or play fields?

» Snow!

DID YOU KNOW?

- Falls Creek is geared towards beginner and intermediate skiers, with around 80 per cent of runs accommodating these types of skiers.
- The longest run at Falls Creek is the Wishing Well (3 kilometres).
- Roughly 4 metres of snow falls each season, boosted by snow-making facilities.
- The village of Falls Creek sits at 1600 metres above sea level.

Halls Gap in the Grampians sits amongst magnificent and majestic scenery. Towering craggy peaks and mountains, lakes and babbling creeks surround the small town, making it the ultimate place to relax. This gorgeous place is a bushwalker's paradise and must-do walks include the Wonderland circuit, the Pinnacle and Mackenzie Falls, or tackle Briggs Bluff or Mount Abrupt. At night indulge in some local produce, and chill out in your villa or camp under the stars. Invigorating, unforgettable.

Miriam Blaker, Hurstbridge, Victoria

» *Feeling the full majesty of the Grampians on top of the rocks*

» *A well-deserved feast in Halls Gap*

GRAMPIANS NATIONAL PARK

Grampians National Park, in Victoria's west, is a magnet for nature and adventure lovers. These expansive, tranquil ranges teem with walking tracks, scenic lookouts, waterfalls, pristine bushland and rugged landscapes, and call to people looking for a dose of fresh air and physical rejuvenation.

The Grampians' traditional owners, the Jardwadjali and Djabwurung people, were displaced in the mid-1800s after the first European visitor, Major Thomas Mitchell, paved the way for graziers to follow in his footsteps. These settlers were followed soon after by fortune hunters when gold was discovered near Stawell. Logging came next, with scant regard for the natural environment and Indigenous camps.

Today, however, the park and the Aboriginal people and their history are protected; the Aboriginal rock-art sites are jointly managed and Indigenous culture is celebrated at the Brambuk Cultural Centre in Halls Gap.

Alongside excellent campgrounds, adventure activities and prolific wildlife, the Grampians also boasts a 150-year-old wine industry, and is home to some of Victoria's most iconic food producers, making it a region that has something for everyone.

Spend a night in the Grampians and watch the sun set over craggy peaks and vast valleys. In the morning, be welcomed by dozens of kangaroos bathing in the early sunlight, then spend the day walking, cycling, driving or climbing your way around the mountains, with the sounds of nature as a backdrop. Visit in spring and you'll witness the ranges covered in a carpet of colour during the vibrant wildflower season.

" The Grampians have such a strong energy about them, and whenever we visit there is always adventure to be had! Whether we camp or stay in boutique accommodation, we always get up at sunrise to experience the magic of the light hitting the rocks, watch the kangaroos bathing in the warmth of the sun, and listen to the music of the birds echoing through the valley. With the smell of the bush, it's a quintessential Australian experience.

Our time here is normally split between trekking and eating! We've had some wonderful afternoons delighting in the local produce at places like Mount Zero Olives and at historic wineries, such as Best's Great Western. And for something a little more formal, a trip to the historic town of Dunkeld was an absolute pleasure. We stayed in the bluestone cottages of Mount Sturgeon, a historic old sheep station, capped off with dinner at the highly regarded Royal Mail Hotel.

No matter what you do in the Grampians, just make sure you find a mountain or even a big boulder to climb up on to feel the full majesty of this truly timeless landscape. "

JEN AND CLINT

PLACES WE GO

WHAT TO DO

- Explore the Grampians by foot on one of the many walking tracks through some of Victoria's most incredible wilderness.
- Bring your mountain bike or hire one locally to explore the national park's bush trails and regional towns.
- Follow a wine-and-food trail to sample some of Victoria's best local produce.
- Visit Billimina Shelter, one of Victoria's most impressive Aboriginal rock-art sites.

GREAT ALPINE ROAD

From wine country to high country, plunging valleys to sparkling lakes, the Great Alpine Road touring route has it all. A spectacular, winding drive through some of Victoria's most scenic countryside, this is a journey that needs to be savoured.

Begin in Wangaratta, sampling fine wines and gourmet produce in the valleys along the road to Bright, ensuring you leave enough time to explore Bright itself, with its fine dining and seasonal beauty. From Bright, climb into the mountain ranges of Mount Buffalo National Park and Mount Hotham alpine resort, a skiing and snowboarding paradise in winter, and a colourful spectacle in summer thanks to its wildflowers.

The route continues on the highest year-round accessible sealed road in Australia, along mountain ridges with numerous hiking and camping opportunities, and then descends into historical Omeo, famous for its gold-rush history and rich pastoral culture. From Omeo, the landscape is tamer, but no less beautiful. With rolling valleys, lush farmland and forest, the remaining leg to Metung takes you over quaint bridges, past wineries and olive groves, and through rustic villages.

It's time to relax when you arrive in Metung (*see* p. 51). Tucked away on a peninsula of the Gippsland Lakes, and with a boutique lifestyle and fishing and boating culture, it is the ideal hideaway to finish your adventure.

There are so many places to stop off along the way, you're spoilt for choice. A favourite stop of ours is the charming town of Bright in the Ovens Valley. With its mild days and crisp evenings, it's been home to many adventures for us, from bike riding to hiking through the valleys, not to mention some wonderful dinners in the restaurants sampling the fine local produce.

We once spent a treasured autumn long weekend meandering along this route. We kicked off with dinner at a Dinner Plain ski lodge, feasting on a roast in front of a crackling fire. The next day we took a leisurely drive to an olive grove near Omeo where we were able to walk through the property and spend time with the owner who had dreamt of planting her trees while on holidays in Greece. Our weekend was capped off with lunch at the Bullant Brewery in Bruthen, where the food was perfectly matched with an array of beers to sample.

The Great Alpine Road is one of those drives that can be filled with your own adventure – as it could mean so many different things to so many different people. "

JEN AND CLINT

PLACES WE GO

WHAT TO DO

- Stop in Milawa, between Wangaratta and Bright, and call in at the Milawa Cheese Company and iconic Brown Brothers winery.

- Break your journey in Dinner Plain, 10 kilometres south of Mount Hotham and an ideal base for snow adventures in winter or horseriding in summer.

- Between Omeo and Metung, stop at Ensay Winery in the Tambo River Valley and Bruthen's Bullant Brewery to sample the local drops.

» *Enjoying Bullant Brewery*

Travelling across lofty mountains and through plunging valleys, lush forests and rolling vineyards along our journey on the Great Alpine Road, we dined on fresh local produce, sampled regional varietals and caught our own lunch by throwing a line in a mountain stream. Driving and cycling along Australia's highest year-round accessible sealed road to experience Victoria's diverse landscapes up close was an absolute dream!

Brian Loughton, Falcon, Western Australia

» *You can travel the road in any season*

This is one of those places where the journey is as enjoyable as the destination. The Great Ocean Road encourages you to stop, breath and enjoy what nature has to offer.

**Veronica Zaitseff, Berala,
New South Wales**

» *Sandwiched between the coast and the rainforest, this is one of the world's most spectacular drives*

» *Flotsam and jetsam on a wild beach*

» *The Twelve Apostles rise majestically from the ocean*

GREAT OCEAN ROAD

One of the most spectacular and dramatic journeys in the country, the 243-kilometre-long Great Ocean Road is an iconic Victorian experience. Stretching between Torquay and Allansford and taking in some of the state's most visited and beloved landmarks, towns and beaches, the coastal route is steeped not only in beauty, but also in history.

Built by returned soldiers from World War I between 1919 and 1932 as a memorial to fellow servicemen who had been killed, it is the world's largest war memorial. Due to the perilous coastal cliffs, bush wilderness and primitive provisions, several workers were killed at task. But there were times when the job wasn't so arduous, such as when the steamboat *Casino* became stranded after hitting a reef, forcing it to offload 500 barrels of beer and 120 cases of spirits. A subsequent two-week-long drinking session ensued when then workers got their hands on it!

This is just one story from the area's rich maritime history, which includes more than 630 other shipwrecks along a notorious stretch of coast. Though dramatic at times, much of the coastline is also home to beaches where swimming, surfing, fishing and simply relaxing are the name of the game. Some of Victoria's most famous coastal towns can be found along the route, such as Lorne, Anglesea and Apollo Bay, which all thrive in summer. The road also weaves through the Great Otway National Park (*see* p. 44), with lush rainforest framing the drive in sections and providing excellent off-road adventures.

Perhaps the most famous landmarks along the route are the natural wonders found near Port Campbell, such as the Twelve Apostles – sandstone formations rising majestically out of the Southern Ocean.

" 'Just keep your eyes on the road' is a pretty common utterance whenever we drive along the Great Ocean Road … As we wind our way around countless bends, twists and turns hugging the rugged coastline, the view outside the window is so commanding, it's hard not to look around when you're behind the wheel. As much as it's stunning, it can also be a little dizzying at times, as you navigate cliff faces that drop steeply to the wild ocean below.

The road has so many beautiful places to stop and take photos. The famous Twelve Apostles are always an eye-catcher. We've seen them from both the side of the road and from a helicopter. The iconic rock stacks rise up from the ocean and the water smashes around them, continually carving out their unique forms.

We've enjoyed many summers and lazy weekends in this part of the world, hanging out at favourite places like Aireys Inlet, Wye River and Lorne, surfing, eating ice-cream and drinking beer at local pubs. We've even participated in the much-loved Lorne Pier to Pub event! I'll never forget jumping off that pier with hundreds of others around me, all scrambling for our patch of water and making the 1.2 kilometre swim towards the pub where we celebrated at the end of the day!

Whenever a friend from interstate or overseas comes to Victoria for the first time, we always tell them to head down the Great Ocean Road. No matter what the weather, it never disappoints. It really is one of the world's greatest drives. "

JEN AND CLINT

[PLACES WE GO]

WHAT TO DO

- Walk all or part of the Great Ocean Walk, opened in 2004 and shadowing the Great Ocean Road through the Great Otway and Port Campbell national parks. There's a choice of camping or luxury accommodation along the way.

- Learn to surf at one of the many surf breaks along the Great Ocean Road.

- Sample excellent fare at numerous cafes, bars and restaurants in the coastal towns and villages along the way.

- Discover important parts of Victoria's history, such as Victoria's first European settlement at Portland, or climb to the top of Australia's oldest lighthouse at Cape Otway, and see for yourself why so many shipwrecks occurred along this treacherous stretch of coast.

GREAT OTWAY NATIONAL PARK

» Facing the famous Great Ocean Road

With a spectacular setting facing Victoria's famous Great Ocean Road (*see* p. 43), Great Otway National Park, or 'the Otways', delivers incredible ocean views, lush rainforest, a rolling hinterland and sparkling waterways. It's one of Victoria's true adventure playgrounds, with superb natural experiences, scenery hard to match anywhere else in the state and one of the world's greatest scenic drives.

The coastal towns attract visitors with their laid-back charm and summer vibe, and are a mecca for surfers and beach lovers who migrate here in the warmer months. The hinterland gives way to some of the best bushwalks in the state, which are rich in wildlife and provide a lush, green and often misty environment. This is a place where you can take a big gulp of fresh, clean air and feel it doing you the world of good.

» Still waters on a dawn kayaking trip

Australia's oldest mainland lighthouse sits proudly at the southern tip of Cape Otway and offers panoramic views of this ruggedly spectacular coastline from the top. Lush waterfalls can be accessed on just a short walk from the road in many places, in settings resplendent with native gums.

Stay a day, or a week, and the Otways will definitely deliver big on 'great' experiences.

> The scenery here is *amazing*. You can camp with the wildlife and go mountain-biking, bushwalking and road cycling to your heart's content. Visit wineries and breweries and taste the local foods. Beautiful beaches are also on your doorstep.
>
> **Tracey Duggan,**
> **Altona Meadows, Victoria**

WHAT TO DO

- Stay in the coastal towns of Lorne or Apollo Bay, or the estuarine villages of Wye River or Kennett River, enjoying the beach and bush by day, the entertainment and dining by night.
- Get a bird's-eye view of the rainforest on the Otway Fly tree-top walk, the world's tallest elevated walkway of its kind.
- Take a walk in the forest and see Hopetoun Falls and Triplet Falls.
- Drive the full length of the Great Ocean Road to experience the dizzying views, dramatic limestone cliffs and turquoise waters of one of the world's greatest journeys.

» Jaw-dropping waterfalls

» *There's nothing like the roar of 100,000 people on Grand Final day*

MELBOURNE CRICKET GROUND (MCG)

The home of Australian sport. Learn about the history of the AFL and all of Australia's greatest sporting memories at the National Sports Museum and then sit back and relax with a beer and a pie to watch a game of Aussie Rules Football. If you are lucky enough, you could cheer on the country's best at the AFL Grand Final, or land a seat during summer to watch the Aussie cricketers take on the world's best teams in big matches such as the Boxing Day test.

Melanie Dunn, Battery Point, Tasmania

It might seem peculiar to classify a sporting ground as a destination, but the Melbourne Cricket Ground (MCG) isn't just any old sports field. It is legendary among sports fans worldwide. Its history includes some of the most dramatic and emotional moments in world sport, and on game day at 'the G', it's hard to beat the atmosphere and exhilaration of being in the crowd at this super stage of sport.

Built in 1853, the MCG is home to Australian Rules Football and the birthplace of test cricket. It hosted the 1956 Olympic Games opening and closing ceremonies, as well as track and field events, and has seen soccer World Cup qualifiers, rugby league and state-of-origin test matches and the 2006 Commonwealth Games.

It's also hosted some of the biggest music concerts in the country, including the Rolling Stones, U2, Michael Jackson and Madonna.

Visit for any reason and the atmosphere of the ground and the 100,000-plus crowd will surround you. Imagine Sir Donald Bradman making a century or Shane Warne bowling a hat-trick. Hear the roar of the crowd on AFL Grand Final day and the iconic final siren. It's the tears that have been shed, the celebrations shared and the honours earned in this stadium that make it Australia's favourite ground.

" How can we possibly go past the MCG making our list? It's part of the tapestry of what makes Melbourne 'Melbourne' – for the city is sports mad. It's a place that's been filled with so many treasured memories for so many Australians, including me.

Like most players and spectators alike, I've certainly shed some tears there. After dreaming of running onto the revered ground since I was seven years old, I was lucky enough to pull on the jersey for both the Melbourne Demons and the Geelong Cats [both AFL teams] and run down the race with my teammates. And I can tell you there is nothing like the chill through your spine when that first ball is bounced in front of a packed stadium of 100,000 people, all there for the love of this great game. "

CLINT

PLACES WE GO

WHAT TO DO

- Attend an Australian Football League (AFL) game or test-cricket match to enjoy the atmosphere of die-hard sports fans cheering on their favourite teams.
- Visit the National Sports Museum, Australia's finest representation of sport artefacts and history.
- Take an MCG tour to learn about the stadium's greatest sporting moments, access the 'backstage' areas and walk onto the hallowed turf.

MELBOURNE

> We live in Melbourne, and yet we are always discovering something new. In a city that is buzzing with a cosmopolitan culture, it's wonderful to explore its many laneways and strip shops filled with cool cafes, restaurants and bars that make up its rich tapestry.
>
> Melburnians love a big event; we come out in droves to enjoy them. We have so many fond memories of celebrating our great sport, music, fashion, theatre, comedy or even fun runs that see the streets come to a standstill – there are just too many to mention! It's no wonder Melbourne has the reputation for being one of the most liveable cities in the world; it really does have a great vibe.
>
> And we'd like to pay tribute to Melbourne's coffee culture, for it's one of our many treasures, and we love nothing more than heading out on a weekend for a long lazy brunch and a great coffee – it's a very Melbourne thing to do, and something we hold dear to our hearts. "

JEN AND CLINT

PLACES WE GO

Melbourne is a buzzing metropolis renowned for its parks and gardens, where contradictions and contrasts are the norm and everything has a place. It's an exciting blend of old and new, where grand Victorian-era buildings sit comfortably alongside modern architectural gems and funky, industrial spaces, and broad, sophisticated, tree-lined boulevards intersect with a labyrinth of cool, grungy alleyways housing 'secret' bars and shops.

Established in 1835 by European settlers from Tasmania in search of pastoral land, it was declared a city in 1847 and eventually became the capital of the newly formed state of Victoria in 1851, transforming into one of the world's wealthiest and largest cities in the 1850s during the gold rush.

The land on which the city of Melbourne sits is the traditional land of the Kulin Nation. Its traditional owners are the Wurundjeri, Boonerwrung, Taungurong, Dja Dja Wurrung and Wathaurung. Historically, Melbourne has always been a kind of meeting place. Indeed, today it is a melting pot of people from all over the world and prides itself on its multiculturalism.

Melbourne is a city famous for its cosmopolitan culture, arts, sport, fashion and food. Voted one of the world's most liveable cities, its residents and visitors enjoy outdoor pursuits despite the often fickle weather. Located on Port Phillip Bay, the beachside suburbs are hubs for dining and physical activity, while the inner-city suburbs are equally popular for boutique and bohemian shopping strips and the popular cafe culture that seems to define most Melburnians' lifestyles.

WHAT TO DO

- Shop till you drop in the CBD's fashion malls, arcades and alleyways, or head out to fashion precincts such as Chapel Street in the inner-city suburb of South Yarra.
- Get your Italian on in Lygon Street, Carlton, Melbourne's 'Little Italy'.
- Head to the vibrant seaside hub of St Kilda, home to the amusement park Luna Park and some of Melbourne's best restaurants, bars, cafes and delis.
- For art and culture, head to the National Gallery of Victoria (NGV), the Melbourne Museum, the Melbourne Theatre Company, the Arts Centre or Federation Square for just a few of the incredible options available.
- Catch an Australian Football League (AFL) game at the internationally famous MCG (*see* p. 47), watch the Australian Open Grand Slam tennis event in January at Melbourne Park, or see the horse race that stops a nation at the Melbourne Cup each November.
- Head to the Queen Victoria Market, Victoria's most celebrated market for more than a century.

Melbourne is a vibrant city of cultural delights, with delectable foods from every country, fashions and fads to rival Paris and London, and a delightful maze of city alleyways. Stepping into this wonderful labyrinth of 'almost-secret' cafes and boutiques, you enter the culture or experience of your choice, as a gentle euphoria mesmerises your every sense. I always leave a little piece of my heart in Melbourne.

**Debbie Kinmonth,
Palm Cove, Queensland**

» *Federation Square is the architectural maze at the heart of Melbourne*

» *Sailing away in search of dolphins*

» *Wake up to the sun rising over the Gippsland Lakes*

METUNG

The morning sun rises over the still water, bathing bobbing yachts moored at the marina in a golden light and waking up the resident pelicans that are lazily floating on the lake looking for breakfast. Morning walkers hit the boardwalk, following it into town for a coffee, while anglers launch their boats into the water at Shaving Point, ready for the day's catch.

Metung comes alive every day with locals and visitors enjoying its enviable position on the Gippsland Lakes – a collection of five main lakes fed by four major rivers in Victoria's east, and the biggest expanse of inland waterways in the Southern Hemisphere. Visit just once and fall in love with the boutique ambience, the boating and fishing lifestyle, and the spectacular scenery that combine to make this a picture-book village.

Situated on a narrow peninsula separating Bancroft Bay and Lake King, you can watch both the sun rise and set over the water from Metung. During the day, spend time in the village enjoying the cafes, galleries and boutiques, or just laze around on the village green, the town's central meeting place. Out on the water, boat to other waterfront villages, sail past a pod of dolphins, or head to Barrier Landing. From here a short walk over the sand dunes will take you to Ninety Mile Beach, where dramatic Bass Strait meets the lakes.

" Metung is a charming village whose history and beauty swept us away. One day while we were there, we headed to the marina at around 7am. The Gippsland Lakes were sparkling in all their glory and there was mist rising off the water. A paddleboarder was cruising past with a dog on her board(!), a couple of anglers were quietly throwing out a line and a few people were tending to their boats, readying for the day ahead.

We jumped on board a beautiful yacht for a day sailing on the water with locals Cam and Sasha, who felt compelled to pack up their lives in Melbourne to live their dream running a charter business on the lakes. They told us how they were drawn to the magic of the place – and you can see why. After sailing for a while, we cut the engine and put the sails up – listening to them flap in the wind and exploring the region with the sun on our backs was pure heaven.

Keeping our eyes peeled for dolphins, we headed for Barrier Landing where we got off and walked over the sand dunes for a delicious picnic on Ninety Mile Beach, which, in contrast to the tranquillity of the lakes, was filled with an immense power.

Later that day, as we strolled along the main street, we chatted to a group of locals, who all told similar stories of how they'd come here and simply fallen in love with the place. As we sat drinking beer at the Metung Hotel that evening, contemplating the wonderful day we'd had, we could totally understand the allure. "

JEN AND CLINT

PLACES WE GO

WHAT TO DO

- Throw a line in from the Metung jetty; even if you don't catch anything, the resident pelicans will entertain you.
- Enjoy a meal and a drink at the iconic Metung Hotel, where watching the sunset from the outdoor deck is obligatory.
- Take a sailing lesson with a local operator. With such a wide expanse of still water at your disposal, it's the ideal opportunity to learn the ropes.

MORNINGTON PENINSULA

Crystal-clear bay beaches, surf beaches, hot springs, strawberry farms, world-class vineyards and restaurants ... all in the one spot! You can't get any better than the Mornington Peninsula. It's such a wonderful place to holiday and caters for all ages. From camping right on the foreshore to staying in luxurious homes, the choices are endless. You'll never want to leave!

Antoinetta Tucci, Fawkner, Victoria

A favourite holiday playground for Melburnians, 'the Peninsula' offers gorgeous bay and ocean beaches, boutique seaside holiday villages, indulgent wineries and lively local markets just an hour's drive from Melbourne. During the warmer months the whole region comes alive with an atmosphere of festivity, and a constant flow of visitors arrives to enjoy the Mediterranean-like coastline, waterfront dining, events and activities on offer.

This area was originally inhabited by the Mayone-Bulluk and Boonwurrung-Balluk Indigenous clans before European settlers arrived and planted much of the peninsula with orchards. Serious farming in the region has now declined, but hobby farmers remain, and there is a local tendency towards sustainable, artisan produce that gives people yet another reason to visit and indulge.

Development here has always had a slightly European flavour, and over a dozen villages along the Port Phillip Bay coastline, including Sorrento and Portsea, offer boutique shopping strips, cafes, provedores and galleries with white sandy beaches just across the road. Accommodation ranges from sophisticated luxury to beachfront camping.

In the hinterland you'll find some of Australia's best dining establishments and the peninsula's greatest concentration of wineries and farm gates tucked away in lush bushland areas such as Red Hill. Charming accommodation options, galleries, spa retreats and microbreweries are dotted in between.

" As Melburnians we have so many treasured memories on the Mornington Peninsula. Where could we possibly start? From lazy days on the front beach at Portsea (or a wild surf on the back beach!) to afternoons enjoying the lively vibe at the iconic Portsea Pub, to heading into the rolling farmland of Red Hill and spending a day at one of the superb wineries with friends. It's a beautiful part of the world, and it's easy to get swept away by its charm.

Anyone we ever meet who lives on the Mornington Peninsula always seems to have that beachside glow about them. They enjoy a gentler pace of life, and many say their day starts with walking the dog on the beach, followed by a coffee and the paper at a beachside cafe.

On a recent trip, we spent a morning at the Red Hill Market enjoying the gourmet produce and handmade crafts from across the region. As we sat sipping our lattes, we bumped into friends from Melbourne, which is a common occurrence on Victoria's treasured beachside peninsula, for it's a place we all love to visit. "

JEN AND CLINT

PLACES WE GO

WHAT TO DO

- Swim with the resident dolphins in Port Phillip Bay, and if you're lucky a cheeky seal might even join you.
- Take a horse trail ride along either ocean beaches or between wineries.
- Sail, surf, snorkel and swim on the 150 kilometres of coastline available on the peninsula.
- Play a round of golf at one of the peninsula's 15 clubs, many designed by the best in the business.
- Take a dip in the natural hot springs at Peninsula Hot Springs, a complex offering open-air bathing pools and spa experiences to revive and rejuvenate.
- Hike one of the coastal walking trails that take you along ocean beaches and through national parks.

» The peninsula is a foodie destination

Colourful bath huts on the beach

» The view from the top

» Bring your winter woollies for a snow camp

MOUNT FEATHERTOP

An epic journey along a rocky ridge, surrounded by breathtaking beauty: climbing Victoria's second highest peak is one of Australia's ultimate adventures. And it is not just for experienced climbers: the summit of Mount Feathertop is actually within reach of most moderately fit people, and is a challenge that can be achieved over a whole day or weekend.

The hike, best done in summertime, begins near Mount Hotham's village and follows the craggy 'Razorback' route along the spine of the Victorian Alps, affording panoramic views over the Victorian High Country that will take your breath away. It's easy to spot the summit: at 1922 metres, its jagged peaks contrast with the neighbouring mountains and their more rounded domes. And when the snow lingers on the summit beyond September, resting in the gullies and giving the appearance of feathers, it's easy to see how the mountain got its name.

The track to the summit via the Razorback dips into a saddle before travelling through low shrubs and snow gums, then hitting exposed bluffs before the peak. The final ascent is steep, but the 360-degree views from the top make every bit of this alpine adventure worth it.

> Climbing Mount Feathertop has been one of our most exhilarating adventures in Australia. We took on the challenge in winter (with our good friend and Everest summiteer John Taylor), when the snow was thick and the air crisp, making for a spectacular view at the summit.
>
> We had plenty of food and water on our backs, and set off up the mountain. After a while we clipped on our snow shoes and continued slowly marching upwards! Running out of time (due to the fact that we were also filming for our travel show!), we quickly unloaded our gear at Federation Hut, and pitched our tent ready for our return from the summit. We were losing light but knew if we moved quickly we'd catch the sunset at the top.
>
> In single file we navigated the Razorback, looking over Victoria's spectacular High Country. And as if perfectly timed, we reached the summit just as the sun was dropping behind the horizon. The sky lit up a vibrant orange colour right across the ranges on one side, and on the other, a full moon was like a shining light to usher us safely back down to the hut.
>
> After devouring a hot cup of soup back at the hut, we camped in the snow, listening to the howling winds cut across the High Country. In the morning the ranges were filled with fresh powder, and Mount Feathertop had never looked more beautiful.
>
> (Please note: climbing Mount Feathertop in winter is for experienced climbers only, and you must be prepared.) "

JEN AND CLINT

PLACES WE GO

DID YOU KNOW?

- You can camp at Federation Hut, situated along the Razorback access route, to break up the journey.
- You can ascend (or descend) via a different route from the Razorback, the Bungalow Spur Walking Track, a very pretty trail that is not as exposed, but is more of a continuous ascent or descent.
- The first European to climb the mountain was Baron Ferdinand von Mueller, who was unaware it had already been named, and proposed to name it Mount La Trobe after Charles La Trobe.

» Jen and JT exhilarated after their night climb

MURRAY RIVER

After the Nile and the Amazon, Australia's Murray River is the third longest navigable river in the world. With wide, open waterways and hundreds of kilometres to explore, 'the Murray' has long been a favourite travel and leisure destination.

Flanked by ever-changing landscapes, including the iconic Australian bush, the Murray travels through some of Victoria's and New South Wales' prettiest towns and villages, but also enjoys long stretches of natural surroundings where the only sound you can hear is the native birdsong.

One of the best things you can do on this watery highway is charter a houseboat. You get a feeling of complete freedom as you float silently along the peaceful river, enjoying nature at its best. Dock by a winery, or throw a line in and catch the resident Murray cod. Be inspired by locals whizzing past on waterskis, and watch the sun set from the roof deck with a barbecue sizzling away.

Follow the routes of old paddlesteamers that plied the river from 1853 transporting wool, grain and other supplies. Or dock in one of the historic river towns such as Echuca or Mildura to experience the boutique cafe culture and many fine restaurants.

Best of all, enjoy one of the finest sleeps of your life, floating peacefully on this beautiful river, and wake up to a soft mist rising from the water, pink sunlight filtering through the native gum trees, and a serene Murray River stillness in the air.

> " The Murray River holds many fond memories for our family; indeed, our nieces and nephew always call it their 'happy place'. We often stay in the historic town of Echuca where we grew up and spent plenty of time waterskiing on the river. One of our fondest memories was when we chartered a luxury houseboat and spent a few days cruising around.
>
> We'd sit out on the top deck in the mornings with a cup of tea and watch the sunrise. You could see the mist rising from the river, smell the eucalyptus trees hanging over the water, and hear the call of the birds waking up for the day. At one point we were visited by a kookaburra who perched itself on our railing! With the continuing flow of the river, life was very peaceful.
>
> Once day broke, though, there was a change of mood. One day we jumped on a jet boat and took to the water with local legend and triple-world-barefoot-slalom-champion Brett Sands. We spent the day wakeboarding, but let's be honest: we were just having a bit of fun on the water while Brett was knocking our socks off with his talent (at one stage he was upside-down!).
>
> There's so much to do in the town of Echuca itself. We've spent many afternoons at the local wineries and restaurants, and always seem to end up back down by the water for that magical hour as the sun sets, and a calm descends once again over the mighty Murray. "

JEN AND CLINT

PLACES WE GO ▶

DID YOU KNOW?

- The Murray River, which first began to take shape over 40 million years ago, spans three states: Victoria, New South Wales and South Australia.
- It's continuously navigable for 1986 kilometres between Goolwa, South Australia, and Yarrawonga, Victoria.
- Including its tributaries, it's the third largest water catchment area in the world, and it provides water to over 1.5 million households.
- There are 37 golf courses along the banks of the river.

The mighty Murray River is one of Australia's greatest treasures. It cuts a path through the stunning Echuca–Moama region and is steeped in history. During summer, the gentle river breeze is punctuated by the toot of paddlesteamers making their way through the beautiful landscape. Of course, I haven't mentioned the waterskiing for adventurers, and for all those with angling in their blood, you are in Murray cod country. This place is so amazing I got married there. Add this location to your bucket list. It will not disappoint.

Sean De Fry, Hawthorn, Victoria

» *Jen finding her 'happy place' on the river*

» *Meandering down the mighty Murray on the grand old dame of the river*

» *It doesn't have to be all peace and quiet!*

Phillip Island is rightly famous for its penguins, but this windswept getaway is much more than just a penguin colony. I always like to visit Cape Woolamai and wander around the sandy dunes and appreciate the spectacular granite formations. There's also Rhyll Inlet, a beautiful blend of mangroves and dunes that is home to many species of birds, including migratory ones that have travelled all the way from the Northern Hemisphere.

Rohan Long, Preston, Victoria

» *Enjoying the vibe on 'the island'*

» *In the treetops at the Koala Conservation Centre*

» *Throw in a line or just enjoy the view*

PHILLIP ISLAND

If an island were built for family getaways, Phillip Island would be it. Many a Victorian has special childhood memories of holidaying on this island, a one-and-a-half-hour drive south-east of Melbourne. And the wonder doesn't stop once you're an adult.

Phillip Island is a natural playground. With 97 kilometres of beautiful coastline, you're spoiled with beaches, bays, blowholes and rocky outcrops that make any day here an adventure. And it doesn't just attract people: koalas, seals, mutton-birds and the island's most famous resident, the little penguin, are all here in their natural habitats, waiting to greet visitors.

Cowes, the island's main town, is a thriving and happy village, especially with the influx of summer tourists. With restaurants, cafes, bars, markets and boutique shops, it is the heart of the island with something for everyone. But all over the island there are gourmet producers, restaurants with ocean views, and quaint beach cafes, all worth a visit.

Between eating and drinking, Phillip Island is packed with things to do. You're never far away from a beach, and world-class surf breaks are at your disposal. Wildlife tours and cruises immerse you in the island's natural environments, and for the more hot-blooded, the motorcycle Grand Prix circuit will get your motor running.

Every evening there's one activity that brings all visitors together, young and old: the Phillip Island penguin parade. Everyone gathers in the beachfront viewing area to watch one of the world's largest colonies of wild little penguins emerge from the ocean and waddle back to their beach burrows for the night. It's a magical procession and a highlight of any visit.

" Phillip Island holds so many great family memories; it always makes us feel nostalgic. A trip to 'the Island', as locals like to call it, is always jam-packed with fun. People come for all different kinds of reasons, as there is just so much to do, but for us it's all about the wildlife – we love how close it feels.

I first saw the famous penguin parade with my mum and dad when I was a young child. When we returned with our daughter, it brought back the same sense of awe I'd felt as a kid. As we watched the darling little creatures waddle up the beach, our daughter Charli whispered: 'Mum, mum! Look … here they come!'. She was mesmerised by them and in absolute wonderment. Phillip Island Nature Parks does a brilliant job in not only ensuring the penguin population thrives, but also educating all visitors in a fun and interesting way.

We've enjoyed so many encounters with wildlife that there are too many to list, but another we loved was walking amongst the treetops at the Koala Conservation Centre. The boardwalks enable you to get very close to the cuddly creatures, an experience that was a real hit with all of us.

Another of our favourite things to do here is to check out the markets. From the farmers market at Churchill Island to the Cowes Night Market in summer, we've enjoyed many a lazy afternoon enjoying the lively vibe. "

JEN AND CLINT

PLACES WE GO ▶

WHAT TO DO

- Visit the nightly penguin parade, the most popular attraction on the island and a world-famous event. Don't miss the fantastic, on-site, interactive visitor centre.
- See koalas in their natural habitat via a series of boardwalks at the Koala Conservation Centre.
- Head to the Nobbies Centre, an interactive visitor centre with a focus on local marine life, from where boardwalks along a spectacular headland lead to views of dramatic rock formations and Australia's largest colony of fur seals at Seal Rocks.
- Fish for rainbow trout at Rhyll Trout and Bush Tucker Farm, straight from its rainforest pool.
- Learn about some of Victoria's European settlement history on Churchill Island, a heritage farm.

WALHALLA

It could easily have turned into a ghost town. Walhalla, a historic and picturesque township nestled deep in Gippsland's scenic Stringers Creek Valley, was once a thriving and rich mining town, home to about 2500 gold seekers in the 19th century. Today its population of around 20 residents keeps the town alive and its history celebrated, but for over 60 years after the last mine closed in 1915, Walhalla was a mere shadow of its former self.

It's hard to believe that this tiny town was once the site of one of Victoria's biggest gold booms. When Ned Stringer discovered gold in 1862, word spread fast, and when Cohen's Reef, the longest single reef in the state was struck upon, the booming region became known as the 'Valley of the Gods'. More than 75 tonnes of gold was extracted from Cohen's Reef. Ten hotels, three breweries and seven churches existed to supply the town's demand, but it was a case of boom then bust. When the railway was built in 1910, it did little more than transport nearly all of the town's buildings and machinery out of the valley after the last mine closed only a few years later.

In the last 30 years, Australians have once again taken an interest in Walhalla. Buildings have been lovingly restored and people are returning in droves, this time to visit the quaint little town and learn about its amazing history.

WHAT TO DO

- Take a tour of the Long Tunnel Extended Gold Mine, the most successful mine of its time, accounting for 50 of the 75-plus tonnes of gold extracted from beneath the town.
- Ride the Walhalla Goldfields Railway, a restored version of the original rail line built to transport gold.
- Stay and eat at the Star Hotel, rebuilt after it was lost to fire in 1951. It was one of the original hotels and today is the heart of the town.

Walhalla is a beautiful historic village set in picture-perfect surroundings. Experience the heady gold-rush days in the charming village, pan for gold in the creek and walk the sheer track up to the cricket pitch. Explore the impeccably restored buildings, such as the fire station, museum, rotunda and Star Hotel, and ride the steam train, which spans the spectacular Thomson River.

Miriam Blaker, Hurstbridge, Victoria

» Strike gold with a tour of Long Tunnel gold mine

» The train that gold built and locals restored

The layout at Tidal River is great – you camp in lovely surroundings with lots of friendly people. Wildlife is everywhere: wombats, rosellas, kangaroos, emus, seals, penguins, possums. You need to be careful that the wombats don't souvenir your bread though! The water is clear and great for kids to swim in, and the walks are fantastic, as are the views. There's a shop for provisions and cabins if you don't want to rough it. If you haven't been here, you are missing out!

Simon Renehan, Rosanna, Victoria

» *Jen letting the magic of 'the Prom' sweep her away*

» *Granite boulders stand watch over the beach*

WILSONS PROMONTORY

Wilsons Promontory, or 'the Prom', as it's affectionately known, has long been a popular holiday destination for nature lovers. At the southernmost tip of mainland Australia, in the state of Victoria, this much-loved national park offers a spectacular landscape where granite mountains meet sandy beaches, and open bushland merges with dense rainforest.

The Prom is one of the largest coastal wilderness areas in Victoria, and has been a national park since 1898. However, Aboriginal occupation of the park dates back some 6500 years and the Boon Wurrung, Bunurong and Gunaikurnai identify the national park as their traditional country.

Most visitors head to Tidal River, the only permanent campground/settlement in the park. Nestled behind the sand dunes of beautiful Norman Bay, Tidal River becomes a small township in the popular summer months, during which time accommodation is balloted. Here you can also find a small selection of wilderness huts and lodges.

Away from the campground, peace, solitude and a natural paradise can be found on the many bushwalks – ranging from a few hours to a few days – available throughout the park. One of the most popular walks is to Squeaky Beach, a moderate hour-long return walk that offers views of the Prom's west coast and a spectacular climb over the headland between Norman and Leonard bays. You then descend to Squeaky Beach where the rounded quartz sand literally squeaks when you walk on it.

Whichever walk you choose, you can trek this pristine wilderness and feel like you have the entire park to yourself.

> Wilsons Promontory is without doubt one of our favourite places to go in Victoria. And the Tidal River campground would have to be one of the most stunning spots to pitch a tent in Australia. There's nothing better than waking up and being enveloped by nature – from the bushland to the white sandy beaches and friendly wildlife.
>
> There are so many different walks, you're really spoilt for choice. We took a leisurely stroll on a track that led us to one of the most southerly warm temperate rainforests in the world, and then made our way up the side of a mountain, perching ourselves on a boulder to watch the sun set over the national park. As soon as we arrived, rays of light beamed across the ocean like a show straight from the heavens.
>
> One of my favourite memories was on Norman Bay beach where we played a game of beach cricket. We had the entire place to ourselves, which was hard to believe because we were surrounded by so much beauty. Just like on a quintessential Aussie holiday, our little *Places We Go* family played cricket till the sun went down. It was the kind of day where we packed the camera up and let the true magic of the Prom sweep us away.
>
> This destination really is world class. Every time we go, we feel like we've been away forever. It's one of those timeless places that has a magnetism that I'm sure is good for the soul.

JEN AND CLINT

PLACES WE GO

DID YOU KNOW?

- The most abundant marsupial in the park is the common wombat. These cute critters regularly visit campsites in their search for food.

- Tidal River leads straight into Norman Bay and swells with the tide, hence its name. It is a purple–yellow colour, thanks to the tea trees in the area that stain it with tannin.

- The Wilsons Promontory Lightstation was built in 1859 from local granite on a peninsula jutting out into Bass Strait. Supplies were shipped to the lighthouse only every six months, and there was no other communication to the outside world for the isolated families who lived here.

YARRA VALLEY

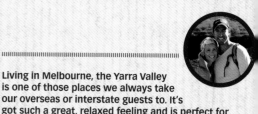

The Yarra Valley is an escape from the hustle and bustle of the city into a world of indulgence. Here you'll find nature at its finest, rolling hills covered in vineyards, world-class food and wine, and an easy, relaxed pace of life.

Just an hour from Melbourne's CBD, this valley is an assault on the senses. The views over the region that pioneered Victoria's wine industry from 1838 include picturesque villages, cellar doors that range from quaint and rustic through to architectural gems, and bountiful vineyards and farmland, with the lush green Dandenong Ranges forming the background.

The area around Healesville, one of the main towns in the region, was originally occupied by the Yarra Yarra or Wurundjeri Aboriginal group. This group then settled at a reservation on nearby Badger Creek, which became Victoria's largest Aboriginal reserve until it closed in 1924.

Today the region's cool climate lends itself to a thriving wine industry, suited to chardonnay, pinot noir and sparkling wine; some of Australia's most iconic wine institutions have been stalwarts in the area for generations. And wherever there is wine, there seems to be food. The areas around the towns of Yarra Glen and Healesville in particular offer many restaurants and artisan producers, creating some of the country's best culinary experiences.

WHAT TO DO

- Let someone else do the driving on a winery tour so you can sit back, relax and enjoy some of the superb cellar-door offerings.
- Stop at Hargreaves Hill Brewing Co in Yarra Glen for an extensive choice of boutique beers and ciders.
- View the valley from the sky on a morning hot-air balloon flight, the perfect way to get another perspective of this beautiful region.
- Book into one of numerous boutique accommodation options. It might be close to Melbourne, but the Yarra Valley is deserving of more than one day of your time.
- Attend any of the regular events the Yarra Valley hosts, such as the Grape Grazing Festival, farmers markets, music festivals held in the grounds of wineries, and annual short and long lunches.

» Some of the valley's spectacular food

Grapes on their way to becoming wine

SOUTH AUSTRALIA

» Historic Adelaide

» Clint at Adelaide Central Market

» *The suburb of Glenelg is a buzzing, beachside location*

ADELAIDE

Small enough to constantly reinvent itself, big enough to offer something for everyone, South Australia's capital is at the forefront of culture, arts, food and events, and it's leaving others behind.

Blessed with beautiful beaches minutes away, world-class wine regions on its doorstep and a pioneering culture that just keeps on moving forward, the city has an immense sense of space surrounding its grand colonial architecture and expansive parklands, so unlike other capital cities. You never feel the hustle and bustle here.

Known as a city that loves to party, the capital is a great host, and lively festivals decorate the city's calendar throughout the year, celebrating food, culture, sport and the arts. Indeed, the locals are a proud lot, and enjoy the healthy competition between other cities and states for recognition of their exports.

The land on which Adelaide stands today was inhabited by the Kaurna Aboriginal tribe, until Europeans arrived in 1836 and proclaimed the province of South Australia. Adelaide was planned as an easily navigable grid pattern and today consists of mostly wide streets around central Victoria Square. On the outskirts is a ring of parklands, keeping the city green.

Its cultural mix ensures there is a plethora of diverse and spectacular dining on offer, and passionate locals guarantee it is always matched with a drop from one of the regional wine districts, such as the Barossa or Adelaide Hills.

You are spoiled for choice in this easy-to-visit city, where recreation is king and there is always something to celebrate.

> " Every time we visit Adelaide, we leave wanting a bit more. We've been countless times to check out the great comedy, music and sport, but we must say, it's the food and wine culture that tops it all off beautifully.
>
> On our most recent trip we decided to stick to a theme of food and wine (which South Australia is so good at!), and a trip to the Adelaide Central Market summed up what South Australians are like. It was like a huge celebration of all the passionate producers from right across the state. Everybody seemed to know each other, and after we'd sampled (and purchased!) their produce, they'd suggest other stalls to go and check out, which made the experience really warm-hearted. To get fully immersed in the market's 140-plus-year history, we couldn't miss a stop at Lucia's, a famous little cafe started in 1957 by Italian migrants.
>
> South Australia really does food and wine so well. We love discovering boutique wine bars, filled with passionate locals, all sharing their love of not only their great wine, but also their beautiful backyard. "

JEN AND CLINT

PLACES WE GO

WHAT TO DO

- Catch a game of cricket in summer or Australian Rules Football in winter at the recently refurbished Adelaide Oval, the perfect place to soak up some passionate Adelaidean sporting culture.
- Hire bikes for free from 14 city locations to explore Adelaide, which is easy to cycle around.
- Go shopping at the Adelaide Central Market, the largest fresh-produce market in the Southern Hemisphere, and over 140 years old. It is the hub of food in Adelaide and a melting pot of cultures.
- Swim with dolphins or learn to sail in the beachside suburb of Glenelg, which comes alive in summer, buzzing with entertainment.

THE BAROSSA

Just an hour's drive north-east of Adelaide, the Barossa is a feast for the senses. Steeped in European and Aboriginal history, today it is a thriving region for world-class wines, artisan food producers and a local tourism industry that flourishes on the combination of both.

The food and wine philosophy in the Barossa is very much guided by the seasons, with passionate producers crafting award-winning products that celebrate the local region, fertile soil, agrarian culture and distinct climate.

It is one of the world's oldest wine regions and boasts around 150 wineries and cellar doors. Many of its wineries are household names, with Jacob's Creek, Penfolds and Seppeltsfield all at home here. The area is famous mostly for its hearty shiraz, thanks to its cool summers and rainy winters.

Before the vignerons moved in, the Peramangk Aboriginal people roamed the region, sharing the northern section with the Ngadjuri people. The area was given its present-day name in the 1830s by Colonel William Light who led the first European exploration party into the region. It was settled in the early 1840s by a Prussian community who were avoiding religious persecution in their own country.

The Barossa's heritage is evidenced almost everywhere you go. Many cellar doors are housed in historic buildings, beautiful Lutheran churches crown small but vibrant villages, and wineries like Seppeltsfield are steeped in traditions, such as releasing a 100-year-old wine every single year.

" We are lovers of food and wine, so you can imagine how much we adored the Barossa. It's absolutely world-class, and spending a leisurely few days driving through rolling vineyards produced that wonderful feeling of enjoying the finer things in life. But it wasn't just the delicious journey we went on that was so memorable; our trip was brought to life by the passionate locals we kept meeting – everyone seemed to have a story about food or wine and loved sharing it!

The Barossa Farmers Market was alive with activity and filled with the freshest seasonal produce you could wish to get your hands on. We shopped with a local Italian chef, Matteo, who runs a cooking school, then had a lesson with him on how to make pasta (never realised how easy it was!).

With so many famous wineries to drop into, you're really spoilt for choice. We decided on Seppeltsfield, which is known as the grand old dame of the region. It has a proud and priceless legacy dating back to 1851 and is one of Australia's iconic wine estates. We luckily got to taste its famous (and sensational!) 100-year-old tawny port.

Our trip was capped off with a 'meet the winemakers' dinner at the historic Kingsford Homestead. Here we got to chat with Stephen Henschke from Henschke wines, who told stories of his family's long history in the region, and their dedication to fine wine. He is just one of the many warm-hearted locals that make the Barossa so loved around the world. "

JEN AND CLINT

PLACES WE GO ▶

WHAT TO DO

- Visit the famous Barossa Farmers Market, a haven for foodies and the best one-stop-shop for fresh local produce and a chat with the locals.
- Stop at any one of the numerous cellar doors for a tasting.
- Join a cooking class to learn how the magnificent local produce is best prepared.
- Drop into Maggie Beer's shop in Nuriootpa. Maggie, one of Australia's most well-known cooks and a resident of the Barossa, sells all of her products here, and there's also a cafe and daily cooking demonstrations.

» Some local award-winning wines

» The sun goes down on fields of vines

Wine, dine, relax and explore. Be as busy as you wish or as tranquil and lazy as required. The Barossa region has many adventures on offer for the palate and the mind. There are plenty of lovely walks, cycling tracks and cultural opportunities, and it's a relatively short drive to Adelaide if you need/want to go there. What I like most about the Barossa region is that anywhere is not too far away, and the locals welcome you as a long lost friend.

Pamela Martin, Kalgoorlie, Western Australia

» *Each vineyard has a story – go and taste them for yourself*

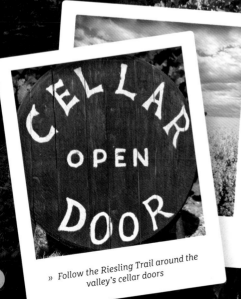

» Follow the Riesling Trail around the valley's cellar doors

» Wine has been flowing through the Clare Valley since 1851

CLARE VALLEY

South Australia is a state that's famous for its wine regions, but each still has its own distinct personality and story. The Clare Valley shines among them, with a rich history and a well-earned place in the international wine industry, particularly for its riesling. It is also a charming and picturesque region, beckoning visitors with its rolling hills, beautiful stone heritage buildings and friendly community.

The Clare Valley is one of Australia's oldest wine regions; vines were first planted here in 1851 by Jesuit priests fleeing Poland, and they have been making wine ever since. With more than 40 cellar doors along a 40-kilometre stretch between Auburn and Clare, the fertile valley produces world-class wines and an exciting food industry based on local produce.

Heritage buildings are still largely in tact, and remind visitors of early European settlers who arrived in the 1840s to share the land with the Ngadjuri Aboriginal people. In 1845 copper was discovered and the town of Burra became Australia's seventh largest town when the world's largest mine was developed here at that time. Pastoral stations with historic homesteads, local halls, churches and cottages all give a glimpse into the past and add to the charm of the scenic valley.

One of the best ways to discover it is on two wheels following the 35-kilometre-long Riesling Trail, which traverses the valley, passing many cellar doors and other attractions worth stopping at.

" We explored the Clare Valley in the depths of winter. First thing in the mornings it was usually a chilly 1°C and the valley was blanketed in a thick mist. But as the sun rose, it unveiled the rolling hills of vineyards, with shards of light cutting across the picturesque valley.

It's hard to know which winery to choose when you're in such an exquisite region. One that we opted for was Sevenhill Cellars, the only remaining Jesuit-owned winery in Australia and one that's full of history. Normally you'd go straight to the cellar door or the tasting rooms of a winery, but we found ourselves sitting inside the stately St Aloysius' Church, soaking up over 120 years of history. Inside the winery museum, also on site, we heard stories about the Jesuits, and how they set up this magnificent winery in 1851 to produce sacramental wine. Downstairs in the underground cellar, still used to store fortified wines, you could smell the history of the beautiful building.

At the cellar door, we relished tasting Sevenhill's much-loved tawny port (and yes, we bought some to take home!), but it was the spirit and warmth of the Jesuit brothers we met that ultimately made our visit so special. "

JEN AND CLINT

PLACES WE GO

WHAT TO DO

- Stop in at Sevenhill Cellars, Clare Valley's original winery, which produces premium white, red and fortified wines. Visit the cellar door and tour the underground cellar and crypt.
- Try other cellar doors too, such as Jim Barry Wines, Knappstein and Annie's Lane, which also have a long history in the region.
- Visit nearby Red Banks Conservation Park, described by palaeontologists as one of the richest megafauna areas in Australia and home to red-earth gorges, waterholes and lush vegetation.

COOBER PEDY

» At the mining museum

In 1915, 15-year-old Willie Hutchison discovered the world's biggest opal field in the harsh Australian outback, 850 kilometres north of Adelaide and 680 kilometres south of Alice Springs. The region quickly attracted settlement from all over the world and became the Coober Pedy Precious Stones Field, and the town of Coober Pedy.

Due to its unforgiving desert location, returned World War I soldiers who came here to mine built their homes underground; they were already used to the trenches of France. Consequently, Coober Pedy became a unique underground city, providing relief from the heat and an extraordinary place to visit.

It is still a thriving and multicultural mining settlement, hosting around 45 nationalities and suppling roughly 80 per cent of the world's opals. Your stay here could consist of a night spent in an underground hotel, exploring the underground opal museum and even attending a service at the underground church. But there's also plenty to experience above ground. Play golf on a grassless course, the only club in the world that has reciprocal playing rights with Scotland's famous St Andrews. Or visit the Breakaways, a unique geological formation of flat-topped mesas that rises out of the arid desert, and was once covered by a vast inland sea.

WHAT TO DO

- Visit Umoona Opal Mine and Museum for a fascinating insight into the region's gem industry and history, as well as its unique underground lifestyle.
- Join the 'mail run', an outback adventure travelling with Coober Pedy's mail-delivery person to see how the bi-weekly run covers around 600 kilometres of incredible outback landscape.
- Visit Faye's underground home. This unique 'dugout', as these types of constructions are known, was excavated by hand by three women 30 years ago using picks and shovels.

" Coober Pedy is a fascinating place to visit. The first thing we compared this hot, desolate outback town to was, strangely enough, an iceberg, for what you can see on the surface is just a fraction of what lies sparkling underneath – in this case, precious stones and the maze of mines and houses that have been carefully carved out of the rock to escape the desert's scorching heat.

We met George, a miner who has been living and working here with his wife for the past 40 years after he emigrated from Greece in his 20s to make his fortune. He says he fell in love with the place, and could simply never leave. A visit out to his mine revealed a man who lives for the thrill of his next 'find'. When I asked him what he has found over the years, he replied, with a twinkle in his eye, 'worth more than half a million dollars'.

George took us down the Umoona Opal Mine and Museum, an old mine that's been turned into a tourism site that gives great insight into this underground world. As we were walking along, we passed opals sparkling in the rock. I asked George if he ever wanted to retire and move somewhere a little cooler. 'Why?', he replied. 'Coober Pedy is home to the good life; the point here is to never judge a book by its cover.' We couldn't agree more. "

JEN AND CLINT

PLACES WE GO

» Mining techniques have advanced in
Coober Pedy's 100 years

» Jen mines the locals for stories
(and they deliver!)

Have you ever wanted to see a wheatfield next to the sea, or spectacular cliffs meeting a rugged ocean? Perhaps you'd like to taste the most amazingly fresh and beautiful Coffin Bay oysters? If so, head to South Australia's Eyre Peninsula. From rugged coastal scenery to quiet bays, friendly locals and impressive national parks, the Eyre has it all. There are plenty of lovely places that you can get to in an on-road vehicle, and also plenty for more adventuresome four-wheel drivers. This is an awesome place.

Marilyn Kent, Dunoon, New South Wales

» *Catch a glimpse of the peninsula's famous marine life*

» *A lighthouse guards the treacherous coastline*

EYRE PENINSULA

They say that wherever there are plenty of fish, there are also plenty of predators, and both are reasons to visit this part of the world. A triangular peninsula with ancient, red landscapes within its interior, and a spectacular coastline teeming with marine life on either side, the Eyre Peninsula is a remote and rugged region, just as famous for its incredible Coffin Bay oysters as it is for its amazing great white shark experiences.

The clean waters of the Southern Ocean around the Eyre Peninsula produce some of the finest seafood in the world, including southern bluefin tuna and yellowtail kingfish; it's no wonder the peninsula is known as South Australia's seafood frontier. And the marine life isn't just good for fishing: spot southern right whales and Australian sea lions off the coast; swim with tuna, giant cuttlefish and dolphins; and come face-to-face with one of the world's greatest hunters, the great white shark, on a shark-cage diving tour from Port Lincoln.

Inhabited by Aboriginal people for many thousands of years, and originally sighted by the Dutch in 1627, the peninsula was not settled by Europeans until 1839. Ironically, whaling and sealing were the region's original industries. Today, these mammals are one of the area's biggest drawcards, for different and much better reasons.

> " Our memories of our time on the Eyre Peninsula will surely stay with us forever, for here we experienced one of the most eye-opening adventures of our lives: cage diving with great white sharks.
>
> In the depths of winter, we joined an expedition from Port Lincoln and took a 2.5-hour boat journey past the spectacular coastal scenery of the lower Spencer Gulf and the islands of Thorny Passage. We arrived at a place called Neptune Island, home to a New Zealand fur seal colony. The seals were basking in the sun on the rocks, and diving into the water playfully.
>
> In these waters, where there are seals, there are great whites, and our time came to see these kings of the ocean up close. We'd been in the cage for just a couple of minutes, when all of a sudden there was a great white staring right at us. It cruised past slowly, then came back again for a closer look. It was about 5 metres long, and never had we been so terrified and in awe at the same time – it was unlike any creature we'd ever seen on a scuba dive before. During our 45-minute dive, we had about 10 sightings; it was truly remarkable. To see these incredible creatures up close, with their massive sharp teeth and powerful bodies, was truly something else. "

JEN AND CLINT

WHAT TO DO

- Discover the main townships: Port Lincoln, Whyalla, Port Augusta and Ceduna, and the coastal and outback communities inbetween. In the west of the region, the only word to describe the landscape is 'frontier', as it gives way to the barren Nullarbor Plain, and the Southern Ocean proves its might along the dramatic stretch of coast.

- Uncover an entirely contrasting environment in the Gawler Ranges to the north, with open plains and pastoral land on ancient landscapes formed by volcanic activity.

- Follow the Seafood Trail, enjoying stunning coastline, incredible seafood and a touch of adventure.

» *Rugged rock formations*

FLEURIEU PENINSULA

Blessed with superb beaches, world-class wineries, exciting cuisine and passionate locals, the Fleurieu Peninsula brings together the best of South Australia in a recreational playground just 45 minutes from Adelaide.

For many thousands of years, this region was home to the Kaurna, Peramangk and Ngarrindjeri people. But in 1802, Matthew Flinders and French explorer Nicholas Baudin mapped the area and Baudin named the peninsula after another French explorer, Charles Pierre Claret, Comte de Fleurieu. The original industries of the region were whaling and sealing, followed by wheat, wool and other forms of agriculture, which is what drives much of the region's economy today.

Both coasts of the peninsula are home to a plethora of spectacular beaches, offering 250 kilometres of coastline for surfing, swimming, fishing, sailing, four-wheel driving and pure relaxation. Rolling green hills dotted with vineyards meet the coastline, and some of the country's best wines can be sampled just minutes from shore in any one of the many cellar doors to be found in the McLaren Vale and Langhorne Creek regions.

Coupled with passionate winemakers is a culture of artisan producers crafting regional gourmet produc matched perfectly with local drops, or indeed to be enjoyed on its own. The strong farming community sustains the region's love for producing local foods, and the Mediterranean-like climate lends itself perfectly to the olives and almonds grown here, which sit perfectly next to gourmet cheeses and freshly caught seafood.

WHAT TO DO

- Visit the wetlands of the Southern Lakes and Coorong National Park, famous for their birdlife, and take an eco-canoe tour to discover this unique environment up close.

- Sample some of the incredible local produce at the regional markets around the peninsula or dine in world-class restaurants inspired by freshness and seasonality.

- Go whale-watching off the southern coast during winter. The southern right whale often comes within 30 metres of the shoreline.

- Stay in any of the seaside towns such as Port Elliot, Port Willunga, Victor Harbor and Carrickalinga for a laid-back beach-oriented break.

- Explore the Mount Lofty Ranges, which traverse the interior of the peninsula and offer a great contrast to the coast, with cool pine forests, waterfalls, wildlife and walking trails.

The Fleurieu Peninsula has it all! Wine, waves and whale-watching. Steam trains, spas and swimming. Fishing, fine food and fitness. Penguins, people-watching and the Port Elliot Bakery. Boating, the Bluff and BMX biking. Cockling, camping and cycling. Galleries, golfing and good times. Come for a week ... or two, to relax and revive.

Lyn Nottage, Victor Harbor, South Australia

» *McLaren Vale has renowned vineyards*

» So beautiful it must be magic: the natural amphitheatre of Wilpena Pound

» Jen and Clint's most scenic campfire yet

FLINDERS RANGES

This ancient landscape is a fantastic spot to camp and ride mountain bikes. You can't help but feel at ease and any stresses melt away as you drive into the rugged mountains. The best time to visit is immediately after rain, when the wildflowers bloom quickly and the creeks and waterholes spring to life. Definitely a place every Australian should visit at least once in their life.

Andrew Leaver, Kersbrook, South Australia

An ancient and unique landscape crowned by the magical, natural amphitheatre of Wilpena Pound, Flinders Ranges is a nature and history lesson rolled into one. Set in the South Australian outback, where the bush meets the desert, the earth tells stories millions of years old. Ruins of farms that have been beaten by the elements exist among vast, rocky plains dotted with gnarled gum trees, acting as reminders of how harsh life can be in terrains like this.

Visitors are treated to incredible visions of nature, especially the ancient mountain ranges whose colours glow in the changing light, and options exist to explore it in many forms. With accommodation options from campgrounds to luxurious eco-villas, Flinders Ranges beckons all kinds of adventurers, especially those with a four-wheel drive.

Farmers battle the elements on cattle and sheep stations, and many have turned their hands to tourism, offering visitors a genuine experience on a typical Aussie farm. Elsewhere, wilderness sanctuaries, such as Arkaroola in the northern Flinders Ranges, have been created to protect local species of flora and fauna, and offer visitors pristine and rugged mountain experiences that almost defy belief.

Flinders Ranges is most certainly worth the 450-kilometre drive north of Adelaide. It's a part of Australia like no other, and is always ready for new explorers.

" The Flinders Ranges are timeless and there's a sense of softness about them, perhaps because of the colours of the sedimentary rocks, which all blend into each other, or the fact that the landscape is millions of years old. Flying over Wilpena Pound, you can see why the meaning of the Aboriginal word for it is 'place of bent fingers', as the mountains resemble the shape of a gently cupped hand.

Rich in uranium, Arkaroola is home to one of the country's most significant geological areas, which dates back to 1.8 billion years ago; it's home to many plants and animals that aren't found anywhere else in the world. Camping here we lost all sense of time, as we set off each day to explore the region. At sunset, as we fired up the barbecue, you could see rock wallabies on the nearby mountain, and the ranges all lit up by the most wonderful glow. "

JEN AND CLINT

PLACES WE GO

WHAT TO DO

- Take a scenic flight over 800-million-year-old Wilpena Pound to appreciate the vastness of the ancient formation and its spectacular surroundings.
- Stay at an outback sheep station to participate in everyday farm activities and learn what life on the land here is all about.
- Test your four-wheel-drive skills on over 100 kilometres of graded roads within Arkaroola Wilderness Sanctuary, one of the best nature adventures to be found.

KANGAROO ISLAND

Australia's third largest island, Kangaroo Island began its modern life as Australia's first free settlement, with sealers, escaped convicts and runaway sailors all making their home here in the early 1800s. It's still a sanctuary today, for both wildlife and people seeking an escape from their everyday lives.

'KI', as it's known to the locals, is a wild and natural paradise where white-sand beaches meet rolling green farmland. Known for the wildlife that roams freely on its shores and its small but passionate community of residents, Kangaroo Island still prides itself on its independence. The friendly locals welcome visitors and proudly introduce them to their artisan food and wine, small, crafty businesses, spectacular scenery and animal friends.

Sea lions, fish, penguin colonies and migrating whales all enjoy their habitats around the island, which is surrounded by the Southern Ocean. Land-based wildlife is also prolific, with wallabies, birds, short-beaked echidnas, koalas and the island's icon, kangaroos, all easily spotted.

The best way to explore is by car. At 155 kilometres long and 55 kilometres wide, the island begs for a driving adventure, on which you can stop and take in any of its natural wonders at a moment's notice and experience the ever-present feeling of complete freedom.

Kangaroo Island is our six-year-old daughter Charli's favourite place in Australia. Countless encounters with the friendly wildlife have left quite the impression on us all actually. It's wonderful to leave the mainland behind and let the ferry transport you across the ocean to an entirely different pace of life, one where nature and wildlife dominate, and the locals are connected to the environment. Driving around the island is an absolute pleasure, especially as there are no traffic lights!

On one trip, we went to the local farmers market in Penneshaw and spent a leisurely morning with passionate producers who make everything from honey to eucalyptus oil to cookies. We did our bit and diligently sampled the various goodies on offer and even tasted figs from hundred-year-old trees (they were delicious!).

Later we were sitting amongst daisies at a wildlife sanctuary feeding grey kangaroos with Charli – as soon as we got the food out, they all came hopping over, as interested in us (and our food!) as we were in them. One of our most treasured moments was when Charli got to handfeed a joey; it was priceless.

By the afternoon we were at Seal Bay, which is home to the third largest sea lion colony in Australia. Watching sea lions come out of the ocean for the night to seek refuge was quite a sight, because they were rolling around playing with each other as they came in, then happily waddling up the beach, seemingly oblivious to our presence.

JEN AND CLINT

PLACES WE GO

WHAT TO DO

- Visit Flinders Chase National Park, home to the lichen-stained Remarkable Rocks, a New Zealand fur seal colony and plenty of incredible bushwalks.

- Get up close to kangaroos and handfeed them at Kangaroo Island Wildlife Park.

- Visit Emu Ridge eucalyptus farm, which produces the only eucalyptus oil of its kind in the world.

- Drop in on the local primary producers who passionately craft Kangaroo Island food and wine, such as Clifford's Honey Farm or Island Pure sheep dairy.

» *Charli had a ball feeding a baby joey*

A hop, skip and a jump from the mainland, yet a world away! Kangaroo Island is full of wildlife, wild unspoilt landscapes, including pristine beaches and native bushland, and sunsets to dream about. There are also many other activities to experience such as tasting wines at local wineries, sampling delicious local produce, surfing and, my personal favourite, getting up close and personal with the wildlife on a guided tour.

Cassie Fuller, Koolunga, South Australia

» *Pass the sunscreen! Basking in the sun at Seal Bay*

» *Blue as far as the eye can see*

Flying over Lake Eyre in flood is truly a once-in-a-lifetime experience. This lake defies logic and fills you with wonder. Not the 'wow, let's take a picture' kind of wonder, but actual heart-thumping, change-your-life wonder. As you admire the gobsmacking size of this body of water lapping a vast desert shore, you get filled with a deep appreciation for the paradox and elegance of nature.

Caroline Pemberton, Manly, New South Wales

» *The best view is from above*

LAKE EYRE

When Australia's largest inland lake is in flood, water stretches as far as the eye can see and you'd be forgiven for thinking it was a mirage in the middle of the desert, with no discernable point separating the water from the sky. And when Lake Eyre is empty, as it usually is, it's a giant salt pan, covering an area 144 kilometres long and 77 kilometres wide, with white crystals that sparkle in the sunlight.

It's one of Australia's true phenomena and is fantastic to see whether flooded or dry, but try to visit when there is some water in the lake, as it's such a rare occurrence; indeed, the lake has only ever reached capacity three times in the last 150 years. When some water does reach it, on average once every eight years, it's a spectacle that needs to be witnessed.

The lake is best viewed from the air; take off from one of the outback towns in the South Australian desert. Looking down over the water, which changes colour with hues of pink, silver and blue, watch the migratory waterbirds that flock here. When the outback rivers flow into the lake it becomes a breeding ground for pelicans, silver gulls, banded stilts, cormorants and ibis, and there's an explosion of new life.

One thing's for sure: when the rains bless the desert and the lake springs to life, it is a pilgrimage every Australian should make.

WHAT TO DO

- Join a scenic flight from William Creek or Marree to witness Lake Eyre – which is spectacular even when dry – plus outback towns and stations.
- Explore the inlets and waterways by kayak, catamaran or small yacht when there is water in the lake.

" We were blessed to see Lake Eyre when it was filled with water and teeming with wildlife. Flying over it was a truly magnificent experience, especially when a flock of pelicans rose from the water and soared through the air. It felt like we were in a David Attenborough documentary when, for a moment, everything looked like it was in slow motion as we hovered over the water that kept displaying an ever-changing rainbow of colours.

When we first drove into the area we almost missed the lake, because it was hard to even see the horizon – the landscape of the salt plains was like a gigantic painting, using a palette of shades of whites and neutral tones.

We stayed in Marree at the only hotel in town, which was a story in itself. The publican Laurie told us how he'd spontaneously bought the pub when passing through with friends one day. The lake was in drought at the time. He said there was barely a tourist in sight, but he loved the old pub and had just retired and thought it might be a nice thing to do. The very next year the rains came and so did the tourists! Laurie said: 'I don't think I have seen so many buses coming in and out of one place during a 24-hour period ever before. I felt like I'd won lotto!' "

JEN AND CLINT

PLACES WE GO

» Standing out amidst the neutral tones of the lake

THE NULLARBOR

Considered by many to be one of the quintessential outback challenges in the country, 'crossing the Nullarbor' is an iconic journey through the heart of some of Australia's harshest desert. The Nullarbor Plain is an area of flat, arid or semi-arid desert between Norseman (Western Australia) and Ceduna (South Australia), 200,000 square kilometres in size and about 1100 kilometres from east to west at its widest point. It is the largest bed of limestone in the world and has a long history of intrepid explorers who have braved the elements to traverse it.

Originally inhabited for thousands of years by semi-nomadic Aboriginal people, the Spinifex and Wangai, it was considered uninhabitable by Europeans. However, they became determined to cross it and the first explorer to do so was Edward John Eyre, who succeeded on his second attempt, which took around four months.

Today, the 1675-kilometre-long Eyre Highway takes travellers on the journey east to west or vice versa, and though these days the road is sealed, the conditions on either side of the highway still require careful preparation, and always create a sense of achievement once the crossing is complete.

The route passes through vast, treeless landscapes with endless horizons. Mobs of kangaroos might be seen lining the road, and subterranean limestone cave formations can be found along the way, presenting as blowholes up to several hundred metres from the coast. Roadhouses with accommodation and camping grounds can be found every 100 to 200 kilometres, breaking up the journey, which includes the longest straight section of sealed road in Australia (146.6 kilometres).

"There was quite the sense of occasion in our car as we took on one of our country's most famous drives. There was barely another soul on the road as we crossed the desert landscape, feeling like explorers with the place to ourselves. It was hard to believe how straight and flat the journey could be and it certainly gave us a sense of just how vast Australia really is.

One person with probably the biggest insight into how revered this stretch of road is was the man behind the counter at the Nullarbor Roadhouse, Adam. He told us he'd been living in Nullarbor along with 11 other people and two dingoes for the past six years. 'It's the people who pass by that keep it interesting', he told us. 'People riding pushbikes, driving tractors, in wheelie bins, on skateboards ... anything you can think of that moves or rolls or wheels, you can see come across here! Also lots of people run for all manner of reasons, including raising money for charity.' Adam also told us how he welcomes lots of Japanese cyclists who are peddling their way around the country as a show of honour for when they get back home.

As we left Adam to serve his adventurous customers, just a few kilometres down the road we hopped out of the car at the head of the Bight, and were treated to a pod of southern right whales splashing around just metres offshore. What a rugged, wild part of the world this is."

JEN AND CLINT

PLACES WE GO

WHAT TO DO

- Take the train! If you're not keen on driving the route, the Trans-Australian Railway crosses the heart of the Nullarbor Plain between Kalgoorlie and Port Augusta.

- Witness the annual migration of southern right whales from Bunda Cliffs along the Great Australian Bight.

- Play the longest round of golf of your life on the Nullarbor Links golf course, the longest course in the world, spanning 1365 kilometres along the Eyre Highway, with one hole in each participating town or roadhouse along the way.

Situated on the Old Eyre Highway, Koonalda Homestead was abandoned in the mid-70s. It's a great place to camp right in the middle of the Nullarbor. You can explore the graveyard where the cars that didn't make it across the old dirt highway came to rest. Stay overnight in the original homestead or in the shearer's hut and experience the true sounds and serenity of the Australian outback.

**Shane Canfield,
Hoppers Crossing, Victoria**

» *There's more to see on the Nullarbor than you'd expect*

Next 96 km

» *It's a straight 96 kilometres from this road sign*

YOU are at: WILLIAM CK.,
(POP. 2) on the
OODNADATTA TRACK

2398 DARWIN		PERTH	3020
880 ALICE SPRINGS		BRISBANE	2442
900 AYRES ROCK / 50 MARLA		SYDNEY	2190
NOTE:'NEW' TRACK ROUTE		MELBOURNE	1780
DALHOUSIE THERMAL PONDS		PORT AUGUSTA	600
(WITJIRA NATIONAL PARK)		WILPENA POUND	500
212 Mt. O'HALLORAN LOOKOUT			FLINDERS RANGES
201 OODNADATTA		MARREE 220	LYNDHURST 300
CAS. HALF ALIVE A?		OODNADATTA TRACK END	STRZELECKI TRACK ENT
156 OCKENDEN SPRING		LAKE EYRE 5TH	CALLANNA / FETTLER'S / WANGIANNA / COTTAGE / MARYVALE / RUINS / IRRAPATANA
147 ALGEBUCKINA		135	'BUBBLER'&'BLANCHE CUP' / ARTESIAN SPRINGS-TURN OFF AT ↓
BIRDSVILLE VIA 'FRENCH' TRACK		BIRDSVILLE 740	COWARD SPRINGS 75
			FLOWING BORE & RUINS
			STUART CK. 135
EXPLORER			CATTLE STN.
via FINKE & OLD 'GHAN' TRACK			

THIS SIGN
WAS ERECTED TO COMPLEMENT THE CONNECTION OF STD. PHONES TO
CATTLE STATIONS & TOWNS IN THE OODNADATTA TRACK AREA
IN JUNE 1987.
AND ALSO TO ALLOW LYNNE & ADAM PLATE OF OODNADATTA'S
PINK ROADHOUSE ...

OODNADATTA TRACK

One of the best outback experiences in the country, the Oodnadatta Track traverses semi-desert country in northern South Australia, and is rich with history, culture and adventure. This iconic outback drive traces an original Aboriginal trading route, and was used by explorers such as John McDouall Stuart in the 19th century. Spanning 620 kilometres of unsealed road between Marree and Marla, it passes through the tiny outback settlements of William Creek and Oodnadatta, skirting Lake Eyre on its way.

The bumpy corrugations, natural potholes and rocky patches in the road add to the experience, but for the most part it is a wide and smooth red-earth track. Numerous artesian springs and waterholes lie along the way, supplying the Great Artesian Basin with water. This availability of water led to the track being chosen for the steam-powered Great Australian Railway and the original *Ghan* route, remnants of which feature along the journey, as do relics of the Overland Telegraph Line, which was erected between 1870 and 1872.

Today the Oodnadatta Track is mainly a tourist destination, providing the ultimate in outback adventure. Under a big blue sky, this golden track opens a window to the past and gives a real sense of outback history.

> This is a way to see the real Australia, without all the tourism and tourists. You'll come across places where real Australians – great Aussie characters – live and work and play, places with unspoilt beauty, flora and fauna.
>
> **Sharon Onyett, Dickson, Australian Capital Territory**

" The Oodnadatta Track really gives you an appreciation of just how big Australia is. Driving along, we spared a thought for all the people – both Aboriginal and early explorers and settlers – who travelled out here without the comfort of air-conditioning, let alone a car.

You can see that same pioneering spirit in the eyes of the locals who call the tiny towns along the way home. We stopped off in William Creek, which is situated near Anna Creek Station, the largest cattle station in the world. At 6 million acres it's larger than many countries! Home to six permanent residents and a dog called 'Pig', William Creek is so small it doesn't even have a postcode! There's not much more here than the William Creek Hotel (where we stayed the night) and a few other buildings.

Inside the hotel we received the warmest of welcomes along with a much-needed cold beer! If you want to know the history of the region, all you really have to do is look at the pub's ceilings and walls, which are covered with anything and everything you can imagine, from stubby holders, to business cards, notes, photos, old hats and even numberplates – anything really, left here by locals and travellers passing through.

We drifted the night away talking to a mixture of characters at the bar. Some were working on the nearby cattle station, others were British backpackers exploring Australia. And then there was the couple, Mim and Bruce, that came here from the city, fell in love with the place and decided to make an adventure of running the pub in one of the tiniest towns in Australia. "

JEN AND CLINT

PLACES WE GO

WHAT TO DO

- Stop in the smallest settlement in South Australia, William Creek, where you might meet all six residents at the historical William Creek Hotel. Food and accommodation is available here, and scenic flights depart from here to Lake Eyre (*see* p. 85).

- Visit the former settlement of Coward Springs, which is now a heritage area and campground that preserves the ruins of an old railway site.

- Stop at any of the lookout points over Lake Eyre, especially when it is in flood, to see one of the world's most fascinating phenomena.

YORKE PENINSULA

Stansbury is a small town on the Yorke Peninsula, about two hours north of Adelaide, that is a quiet place to retreat from the rat-race that is life. When we go there for a long weekend or midweek escape, cards are played, books are read, fishing is done, laughs are had and fun is always on the table. Relaxation is what we feel when we are there.

Leanne Bates, Two Wells, South Australia

Where coastal paradise meets rolling farmlands, the boot-shaped Yorke Peninsula is a welcoming and soothing holiday playground west of Adelaide that offers a carefree, family friendly environment that everyone will love.

With Gulf St Vincent on the east of the peninsula and the Spencer Gulf on the west, you are surrounded by 700 kilometres of coastline offering the very best in fresh seafood. Holidays can be spent choosing between crayfish, scallops, crabs, prawns, oysters and prized King George whiting, creating the best seafood feast imaginable. Catch it yourself or let others do the work; either way, the resulting meal will be scrumptious.

Surfing the Yorke Peninsula waves remains one of the drawcards of the area, and divers relish exploring the shipwrecks off the coast. Otherwise, life here can be as simple as a game of cricket on one of the magnificent beaches.

This was originally the land of the Narungga Aboriginal people, whose descendants still live on the peninsula. European settlers arrived around 1840 when the copper boom was just around the corner, creating the area known as the Copper Coast, which included the settlements of Wallaroo, Kadina, Moonta, Paskeville and Port Hughes. Mining continued here into the early 20th century, contributing to South Australia's prosperity, and historical artefacts from the industry remain as reminders of the area's copper-mining past.

Elsewhere on the peninsula, agricultural trade exploded, with barley being the major crop, as it still is today. Indeed, most glasses of Australian beer will contain Yorke Peninsula barley.

» *The peninsula's pristine beaches*

WHAT TO DO

- Explore South Australia's pioneering history at any number of museums on the peninsula that pay homage to the area's copper and agricultural heritage.
- Go fishing, one of the most worthwhile pursuits on the peninsula.
- Take an Aboriginal cultural tour around the peninsula, following in the footsteps of the Narungga people.
- Get a behind-the-scenes glimpse into life on a Yorke Peninsula farm on the Home Grown Trail. You can visit working farms and studs, and watch shearing, sheepdogs and horse training in action.
- Jump aboard the Moonta Mines Tourist Railway, which visits the major heritage sites around the former copper-mining region.

WESTERN AUSTRALIA

» The impressive full-scale Amity

» Having a whale of a time at Whale World

» If you're lucky, a whale and her calf will come right up to your boat to say 'hi'

ALBANY

On the southern coast of Western Australia, Albany is framed by the sparkling Southern Ocean and the majestic Stirling Ranges. Visitors and locals flock to its wide, pristine swimming beaches, or gather at the local farmers market where gourmet produce is proudly on offer. Down at the pier, anglers return with their daily catch, which might include crabs, snapper and flathead, and between June and October boats head out onto the ocean to spot the pods of whales that return here each year.

Also every year, from around August to December, the south-west region around Albany is carpeted in a sea of wildflowers, an absolute spectacle for the eyes. World-class wineries surround the town too.

The town itself has been shaped by its monumental history. It was the site of the first European settlement in Western Australia, making it the oldest town on the west coast; its heritage can be easily gleaned on a tour through town where there are still more than 50 buildings of historical significance. It was also the port from which World War I soldiers left, bound for Gallipoli. For these men, Albany was the last glimpse they had of the Australian continent, and the country's Anzac history is celebrated and commemorated in Albany more than almost anywhere else in the land.

WHAT TO DO

- Visit the *Amity*, a full-scale replica of the ship that brought Albany's first settlers to town in 1826.
- Join a whale-watching cruise between June and October to spot southern right whales in their annual nursing grounds.
- Go to Whale World, where there's an interesting account of Albany's whaling history, which ceased in 1978. The town is now focused on the conservation and enjoyment of these majestic deep-sea mammals.
- Take a hike in nearby Torndirrup National Park, one of the most popular in the state, with wildflowers, wildlife and bushwalking trails.

Albany is just a small and humble gem in Western Australia's south-west, yet it packs a huge punch with its beautiful, flawless beaches, rocky landscapes and lush green hills. A place of quiet contemplation and adventure, it will leave you hungry for more nature and soul-searching. Everyone needs to experience being on top of 'the Gap' [a rock formation in Torndirrup National Park], looking down over icy-blue crashing waves with nothing between you and the ocean and feeling infinite!

Kathrina Toh, Parkwood, Western Australia

» *Sunset over the Indian Ocean*

" It was a moving experience to walk along the beach at Albany and take a moment to think of the Anzacs who left these shores and sacrificed their lives for our country, and to know that this was the last place they saw before departing for Gallipoli … It was also moving to look out over the Southern Ocean and consider that Albany was the last place in Australia to shut its whaling station down. But full credit must be given to this town – for today whales are not only protected here, they contribute to a thriving tourism industry.

There are not many places where you can walk five metres from your campground and watch two southern right whales frolic in the waves just offshore. And it got even better than that! We joined a whale-watching cruise and just as we were about to call it a day after spotting a few whales at a distance, our skipper John started playing 'Danny Boy' on a wooden flute. Within minutes, a whale came right up to our boat, then went under it and around it, as though it was playing with us. Then, after we'd all taken our photos and watched in awe, it simply swam off without a care in the world. "

JEN AND CLINT

PLACES WE GO ►

BROOME

The remoteness of Broome, in the far north of Western Australia, is part of its allure. Hours from most Australian capital cities, it's the southern gateway to the magical, mystical Kimberley region, where red desert meets white sand and turquoise waters.

Built on the pearling industry in the 1880s, Broome attracted people from many different cultures intent on finding their fortune, which shaped the town's current multicultural and vibrant population. Most importantly, it has an extremely rich Indigenous history, and is home to the Yawuru people.

It's also home to one of Australia's most iconic stretches of sand – Cable Beach – which is where you'll find the famous camel trains, now a symbol of the thriving tourist industry in the area. Don't miss sitting on Cable Beach at sunset, watching the sun dip spectacularly into the Indian Ocean, turning the water into a pool of reds, oranges and pinks, and the camels into mere silhouettes.

Stay a week in Broome at one of the many beach resorts, or just a day before or after an adventure in the Kimberley. Whichever you choose, you'll always leave hoping that you'll one day return.

" I'll never forget the first time I saw Cable Beach with its pristine strip of white sand and famous turquoise waters. We had literally just jumped off the plane and found ourselves crashing through the waves – the sand under our feet was so soft, and the water so clean and clear. I remember thinking we had landed in paradise.

As if that wasn't good enough, the sunsets on Cable Beach were out of this world. Just as the sun started to dip into the ocean, we did the touristy thing and jumped on board the camel train. We watched the sky light up with the most magnificent colours – pinks, oranges, yellows, finishing with a vibrant red – and the reflections in the water as the waves rolled in were magical.

In town you can't miss the importance of the pearling industry, and there's plenty of opportunity to buy a precious Australian South Sea pearl. We took it one step further and explored the waters of the Willie Creek Pearl Farm, where our guide gave us an insight into the modern cultured pearling process. We watched as the technicians seeded a live oyster to produce a stunning pearl!

Every day we spent in Broome ended at a sunset bar down on the beach, watching the magnificent colours in the sky light up this incredible part of the world. **"**

JEN AND CLINT

PLACES WE GO

WHAT TO DO

- Visit Matso's Broome Brewery, known for its unique and imaginative beers that bring people together.
- Drop into Willie Creek Pearl Farm and discover how the rare Australian South Sea pearl is produced, or visit two of the last surviving pearl luggers in the heart of Broome's Chinatown for an insight into the town's fascinating pearling heritage.
- Witness the 'Staircase to the Moon', a natural phenomenon that occurs between March and October when a full moon rises over Roebuck Bay's mudflats, creating an optical illusion of a staircase leading to the moon.

» Jen's hunting for pearls!

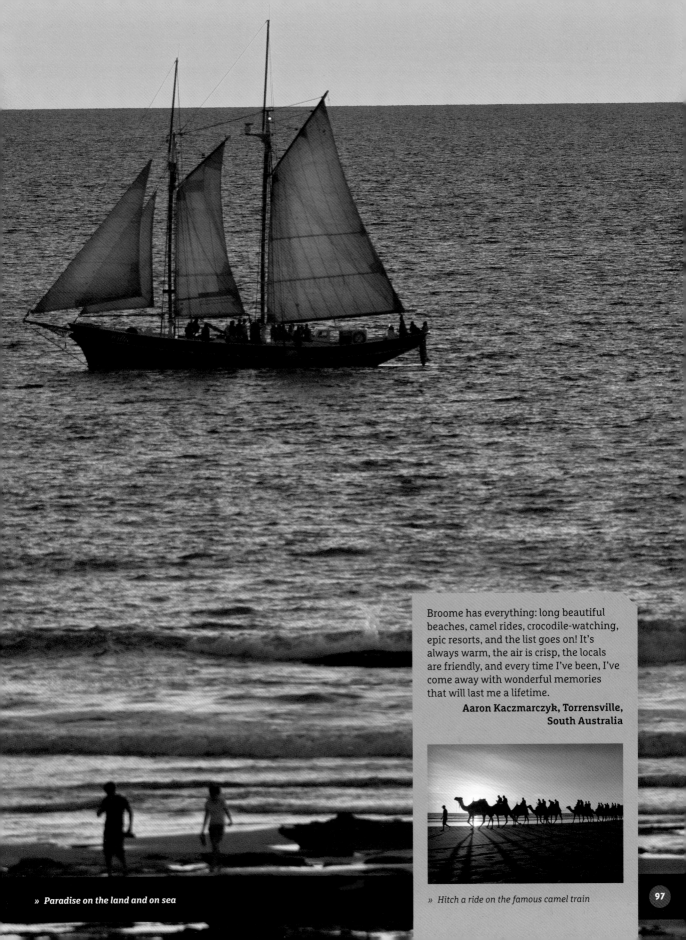

Broome has everything: long beautiful beaches, camel rides, crocodile-watching, epic resorts, and the list goes on! It's always warm, the air is crisp, the locals are friendly, and every time I've been, I've come away with wonderful memories that will last me a lifetime.

Aaron Kaczmarczyk, Torrensville, South Australia

» *Paradise on the land and on sea*

» *Hitch a ride on the famous camel train*

The Bungle Bungles are remote and difficult to get to, but they're worth the effort and challenge. Coming across the orange-and-black, tiger-striped domes is a fascinating sight that leaves you in awe. Travelling further onwards is well worth the effort too, with gorges, waterfalls and tropical pools lined with palms making for a rewarding experience.

**Debbie Westwell,
Gold Coast, Queensland**

» *Silenced by Cathedral Gorge*

» *These ancient 'beehive' domes will take your breath away*

BUNGLE BUNGLE RANGE, PURNULULU NATIONAL PARK

» Happy tourists!

In World Heritage–listed Purnululu National Park in the Kimberley region of Western Australia, the Bungle Bungles rise out of the ground to create a geological landscape so unique, it can literally take your breath away.

It's hard to believe that these magnificent orange-and-black striped 'beehive' domes were largely undiscovered by Europeans until the 1980s. Aboriginal people, on the other hand, have been using the region for sacred rituals for around 20,000 years. According to Dreamtime legend, the domes were formed by the Rainbow Serpent as it slithered across the land.

A scenic flight is one of the best ways to discover this natural wonder, a landscape that is more than 350 million years in the making. Gazing at the scenery from the air, the Aboriginal significance is important to keep in mind.

On the ground, you can experience the majesty of the formations up close, brushing shoulders with the enormous domes as you weave your way deeper among them. Around every corner is another postcard-perfect scene, where the brilliant orange of the rocks seems to glow against the bright blue background of the sky.

WHAT TO DO

- Take a scenic flight either by light aircraft or helicopter over the magnificent domes.
- Book a walk with an Aboriginal guide to bring the range's 20,000-year Indigenous history to life.
- 'Glamp' overnight in bush luxury at the Bungle Bungle Wilderness Lodge.
- Take one of the many hikes on offer to discover the natural highlights up close.

" The Kimberley is a place that has captured our hearts. There's something about the incredible red rocky escarpments that go on forever; they're timeless. And the Bungle Bungles are one of the many treasures that make up this jaw-dropping landscape. I can see why they were one of Australia's best-kept secrets until the 1980s – they're practically hidden at ground level.

Driving into Purnululu National Park, we navigated our way over undulating dirt tracks and several creek crossings. When we arrived at the Bungle Bungles, it wasn't until we took a scenic flight over them that their true marvel was unveiled – perfectly shaped domes that rise out of the earth in such a mysterious way.

Later, on foot, we craned our necks as we walked in silence between the ancient rocks, astonished by the sheer magnitude of the place and mesmerised by the orange-and-black sandstone domes.

Visiting Cathedral Gorge, a huge natural amphitheatre inside the Bungle Bungles, was a really spiritual experience for us. We were lucky enough to have the place to ourselves. I was lying on the sand looking up at the ancient rocks and got lost in thought, wondering who had been here over the thousands of years before us. The energy of the place was overwhelming. I experienced such silence, and such peace.

As night fell, the stars lit up the sky and we camped in luxury tents at the Bungle Bungle Wilderness Lodge. We listened to stories from some of the guides who had come here, fallen in love with the place and couldn't leave. "

JEN AND CLINT

PLACES WE GO

CAPE LEVEQUE

» Check out the view from up here!

Tucked away on the tip of the Dampier Peninsula in the far north of Western Australia, Cape Leveque might be a remote destination to access, but it's certainly worth the effort. Fly or four-wheel drive the 220 kilometre journey north of Broome and arrive in a world of stunning, secluded beaches, red rocky cliffs, and rich Indigenous culture and history.

The area is home to the Bardi Aboriginal people, who named the peninsula 'Ardi', meaning 'heading north'. Many small Aboriginal communities live here today, and some take an active role in welcoming visitors and teaching them their important local culture.

Days here are also spent enjoying the unspoilt beaches, perhaps looking for mud crabs, exploring the reef at low tide or spotting humpback whales on their yearly migration. Don a snorkel and look for turtles and tropical fish just offshore, or take a self-guided walk in the area to discover the local flora and fauna.

At dusk, watch the sun as it drops into the Indian Ocean to create a spectacular Kimberley sunset, making the water sparkle and the red rocks glow.

» Look for mud crabs at low tide

Cape Leveque has it all: great camping, whale-watching, fishing, four-wheel driving to name just a few of the things you can do here. The scenery is fantastic, with blue water, red cliffs and great sunsets. And you can't go past the happy hours with friendly campers who have made the trip north from Broome.

Geoff Cook, Kingscliff, New South Wales

WHAT TO DO

- Take an Indigenous-guided bush-tucker tour, or learn about ceremonial spear making.
- Launch a kayak from almost anywhere on the beach, and at high tide anchor it to snorkel in the warm, clear waters.
- Take a scenic flight over the Buccaneer Archipelago, a rugged area off the coast with around 1000 islands.
- Stay at the Aboriginal-owned Kooljaman wilderness camp for an incredible eco-experience on the beach.

The one thing that struck me about Eco Beach was how soothing it was; the stillness and peace there is overwhelming. You are, and feel, miles away from anywhere and completely in harmony with the earth. With environmentally friendly accommodation tucked seamlessly into the natural landscape, yoga classes overlooking the beach each morning, and, of course, that magical sunset over the Indian Ocean every evening, this is a place of pure relaxation and rejuvenation that will always warm my soul.

Emma De Fry, Hawthorn, Victoria

» Watch the whales migrate south

ECO BEACH

It is not a town, nor even a village, but it is most certainly a destination. Eco Beach, an eco-resort set up on the shores of paradise, is just over an hour south of Broome, where the southern Kimberley's red desert meets the aqua Indian Ocean.

Featuring stylish eco-villas and eco-tents, all set within a stunningly pristine coastal environment, Eco Beach is more than just a resort: it offers a complete immersion in unique wilderness, miles from civilisation.

Walk onto the wide and expansive beach where turtles might also be wandering. Take a guided fishing trip where the locals will show you the best spots for catching the revered barramundi. Kayak on top of emerald waters and discover coves and beaches completely devoid of other humans. Or head out on a whale-watching cruise to spot the local Kimberley humpbacks as they migrate their way back to Antarctica.

And as the sun drops into the Indian Ocean, enjoy the spectacular Kimberley sunset before being welcomed by thousands of stars in the moonlit sky.

> " Even though Eco Beach is only about an hour's drive from Broome, it felt like we were a million miles from anywhere, so you can imagine how it was staying in luxury eco-tents right on the beach!
>
> On the day we arrived, we couldn't believe how turquoise the water was. Framed by silky smooth white sand and a massive blue sky, it felt like the light was playing tricks with our eyes. I remember taking a stroll along the beach and bumping into a park ranger who was helping a giant turtle back into the ocean. This care for the marine life and environment pretty much sums up what Eco Beach is about.
>
> We took to the waters with local guides David and Fiona who not only lead whale-watching trips, but research and record the whales' movements. It was without doubt one of the most thrilling whale-watching adventures we've ever had. We were right in the middle of the Kimberley humpbacks' migration south, so it felt like they were everywhere. I remember hanging over the side of the boat, watching the sunset and remarking on how blessed our day had been, when a massive humpback rose from the water not even a metre from my arm. It gave me the fright of my life! To be up close to these magnificent creatures is an unbelievable experience. "

JEN AND CLINT

PLACES WE GO

» *Sunset over paradise*

WHAT TO DO

- Begin your day with beachfront yoga, welcoming the sun as it rises behind you in the desert.
- Order a picnic hamper and enjoy it on a deserted beach sheltered by the red Kimberley cliffs.
- Join an Indigenous cultural tour and be welcomed to the country by a traditional landowner before exploring the history and stories of the area.

EIGHTY MILE BEACH

Travelling along the Great Northern Highway between Port Hedland and Broome, many people would simply pass this secret paradise by without knowing what they were missing. Just 13 kilometres off the highway is Cape Keraudren Coastal Reserve, comprising 4800 hectares of perfect coastal wilderness including part of the spectacular Eighty Mile Beach – which, incidentally, is actually 140 miles (225 kilometres) long, and, at points, 100 metres wide.

This is where the Great Sandy Desert meets the Indian Ocean, and what a special meeting that is. There are clear, turquoise waters and white sandy beaches for as far as the eye can see. With beachfront sites up for grabs, this is a camper's paradise.

Eighty Mile Beach is particularly renowned for its fishing, and while you're waiting for a catch, some of the best birdwatching opportunities are all around you, as the site has been classified as an Important Bird Area for migratory shorebirds.

Traditional ownership of the land is shared between the Nyangumarta and Karajarri people. In the Karajarri language, Eighty Mile Beach is called 'Wender', which means 'creaking noise' for the sound the dry sand makes when you walk on it. Behind the miles of beach, the land primarily belongs to four main pastoral leases, operated as cattle stations. But the main attraction is the Indian Ocean, and when the sun sinks into the sparkling water and sets the sky ablaze with colour, there are not many other places in the country you'd rather be.

As we set up our caravan, we chatted to fellow campers who had, in fact, been here for three months! They told us that they had almost driven past the place 15 years ago, but had decided to visit as a last-minute stop-off – and have returned every year since. It's that kind of place and its beauty is hard to describe. The dividing line between the Kimberley and the Pilbara, its remoteness adds to its allure, as does the fact that the sky and ocean seem to blend into one.

Up to watch a spectacular sunrise, we met the local park ranger Keith who had been here since the late '80s. He told us how he loves the isolation and solitude. As we walked along the beach, which is surrounded by coral reef, there wasn't another person in sight. There were no tyre tracks either, and no pollution.

As we sat around our caravan at the end of the day, watching our fellow campers fishing for their dinner, they said to us: 'Don't tell anyone about this place; it's too beautiful to be shared.' But we know that if you were driving past the turn-off, you wouldn't want to miss this magical slice of Western Australia. "

JEN AND CLINT

PLACES WE GO

WHAT TO DO

- Camp at one of the caravan parks or bush campgrounds along Eighty Mile Beach and enjoy one of the best sunsets in the country from your campsite.
- Take one of the walking tracks through Cape Keraudren Coastal Reserve to discover the prolific native flora and fauna.
- Drop a line in and try to catch some local threadfin or salmon.

» *It's a spectacular place to camp*

Eighty Mile Beach is a stunning place. It is almost a spiritual experience to walk alone along its massive expanse of sand when the tide is out. And the multitude of shells would keep a beachcomber happy for hours! Just when you think it couldn't get any more peaceful, it's time for sunset, which is magnificent, especially when the tide is out and the sun's rays ripple across the sand flats.

Roz Bayliss, Brisbane, Queensland

» *Detour down the little-marked road to discover Eighty Mile Beach*

» *The best time for exploring is when the tide is out*

El Questro Wilderness Park is a stunning outback experience that everyone should experience at least once in their lifetime. With outstanding landscapes, from sandstone ranges to rainforest hideaways and gorges with the most beautiful waterfalls, there are certainly many adventures to be had here as well as an abundance of wildlife to admire.

Zoey Grafham, Midland, Western Australia

» *Your adventure starts here*

» *A famous boab tree*

» *No, Jen and Clint didn't catch any fish – but they did catch the El Questro bug!*

EL QUESTRO WILDERNESS PARK

This is a destination that doesn't discriminate. Located in the Kimberley region, El Questro Wilderness Park boasts more attractions and things to do than a theme park, offers a level of accommodation for every budget and taste, and doesn't hold back on beauty.

Approximately an hour from Kununurra which is the eastern gateway to the Kimberley, El Questro can be accessed by two-wheel drive and offers a true wilderness experience with as much comfort as you wish.

With accommodation ranging from campsites and permanent eco-tents to a luxury homestead frequented by movie stars, El Questro creates its own holiday community. Travellers of all kinds come together to appreciate and enjoy the treasures that are found within its million-acre boundary, most of which are still undiscovered.

Hike to spectacular Emma Gorge, a swimming hole beneath a waterfall and towering cliffs, or discover tranquil Chamberlain Gorge, which is only accessible by boat along a three kilometre natural waterhole. With vast Kimberley landscapes best explored on horseback, fishing spots best reached by chopper, and natural thermal springs where you can soak your cares away in the middle of nature, El Questro teems with options to explore one of Australia's last frontiers.

> "Being at El Questro felt like we'd stepped onto a movie set that typified what the Australian outback looks like. We were surrounded by massive red rocky escarpments, lush gorges, wide open expanses of land that felt like they went on forever, and those magical Kimberley sunsets that stay with you long after you've left.
>
> We took an early morning horseride around the property and within minutes of leaving the stables it felt like we had the whole place to ourselves. All we could hear was the sound of the horses breathing and bird calls echoing through the valley as the sun came up. We rode to the top of a hill and took in the magnificent Australian outback.
>
> There was no better way to get the lay of the land than via our heli-fishing expedition. While the aim was to catch fish, it was the chopper ride over the rivers and gorges that captured our imaginations. We were flying between giant red towering cliffs and hovering over the water, dwarfed by the rocks all around us.
>
> After half an hour or so, we landed beside a river – I couldn't tell you where that river was exactly, but that was the point. Surrounded by a million acres, we were lost in the beauty of this incredible country. And no, we didn't actually catch a fish … but did we care? Not a bit.
>
> No words will ever do this place justice – you just have to go there!"

JEN AND CLINT

PLACES WE GO

WHAT TO DO

- El Questro extends approximately 80 kilometres north–south and 60 kilometres east–west, a total of around one million acres.
- The property boasts four major river systems, where you can find an abundance of wildlife.
- Many areas of the property are yet to be discovered, so take a scenic helicopter tour and see if you can uncover a new gorge or waterfall.

GIBB RIVER ROAD

» The famous prison tree

A legendary track that cuts through the heart of one of Australia's final frontiers, the Gibb River Road is the gateway to all the adventures that Western Australia's Kimberley has to offer. Stretching around 660 kilometres from Derby to Wyndham, it is the off-road option of the two routes through the Kimberley (the other being the sealed Great Northern Highway) and is accessible to four-wheel-drive vehicles only.

Work began on the Gibb River Road in the 1960s, when it was used to transport cattle between stations. Many Aboriginal people were forcibly removed from their land and treated as criminals during the construction of the road, which lead to the demise of their societies. Today, Indigenous communities have been re-established along the Gibb River Road, and it's important for anyone travelling through the area to respect their heritage and that dark period of history.

Once you get onto the rugged, red dirt of this road, the Australian outback lays itself bare before you. With vast, wide-open spaces all around, the occasional boab tree and no hint of civilisation, it's hard to believe that hidden treasures, incredible history and epic adventures lie waiting to be discovered.

For intrepid travellers with plenty of time up their sleeves, this road offers one of Australia's last true outback adventures. With gorges, waterfalls, natural swimming holes, ancient mountain ranges, caves, rivers and outback cattle stations to explore, it is easy to switch to 'Kimberley' time and let yourself get lost in the rich, red environment.

" Our journey on the Gibb River Road was as thrilling as it was intriguing. As soon as we hit the red dirt, we were thankful for our very sturdy four-wheel drive that enabled us to experience the track without incident! Not to mention our passionate guide Digger who navigated us over the bumps!

To be travelling along such a famous old cattle route in the dusty heat of the Kimberley gives you an overwhelming sense of the Australian outback, where million-acre properties become the norm. With not another car in sight, you certainly wouldn't want to break down out here. Digger enthusiastically shared the rich history of the region, both Aboriginal and European. He talked of the famous Jandamarra armed conflict in the area when settlers came in, and showed us a big old boab tree that was used as a prison, which was a sobering moment.

We often pulled over to the side of the road and turned the engine off just to take everything in. All we could hear was the sound of the wind cutting across the outback. This landscape is so inhospitable, yet so beautiful. "

JEN AND CLINT

PLACES WE GO

WHAT TO DO

- Choose a camping ground, wilderness safari camp, homestay or luxury homestead to stay at along the road (prior bookings are essential).
- Don't miss Windjana Gorge, Bell Gorge, Tunnel Creek, Home Valley Station and El Questro Wilderness Park (*see* p. 107), all located along the route.
- Take an organised group tour if you are not a confident four-wheel driver. Knowledgeable guides on these tours take care of everything and you'll experience all of the highlights in custom-built vehicles.

This isolated road has many gorges and fantastic mountains along its length and is a challenge in itself. There are some great spots to camp beside waterways, and with places like El Questro, Windjana Gorge and Tunnel Creek (renowned hideout of the Indigenous insurrection leader Jandamarra), it is a must-do. The unusual and magnificent boab trees are a sight to behold, including the historic 'Prison Tree' near Derby. Australians love to conquer a four-wheel-drive track and Gibb River Road is definitely one to test.

**Raymond Pearson,
Herberton, Queensland**

» *A natural swimming hole hidden amidst the rugged red dirt*

» *Jen conquering the Gibb River Road*

What a magical place! Karijini National Park never fails to amaze. The colours are incredible, from the bright-red Pilbara dirt to the blue skies and emerald-green swimming holes. With starry skies at night, it is truly a hidden oasis. The gorge walks are spectacular and a photographer's dream. It's the perfect place to take a break from the 'real world' – no mobile reception here!

Francesca Codispoti, Eden Hill, Western Australia

» *It's hard to capture how beautiful it is on camera*

» *You won't be able to resist a swim in this oasis pool*

KARIJINI NATIONAL PARK

An adventure playground, Karijini National Park in Western Australia's Pilbara region is packed full of as many gorges, waterfalls and natural swimming holes as you could fit into the state's second biggest national park.

With rocky, red escarpments, big blue skies and native bushland, Karijini has a rugged beauty that is unique to Australia's north-west. Around 1400 kilometres north of Perth, the national park is a true outback destination, and will entertain nature lovers for days on end.

The park is set on the Hamersley Range, which began to take shape as long as two billion years ago. Today you can glimpse unique land formations and dramatic gorges and valleys that have been carved over hundreds of millions of years from numerous lookout points offering panoramic views. Further superb Pilbara views reward those who climb to the top of Mount Bruce, the state's second highest mountain.

But to experience Karijini's magic to the full, it is all about exploring the details. Hike into the plunging gorges, cling to rocky ledges and discover natural spa pools perfect for swimming. Keep your eyes peeled for kangaroos, rock wallabies, dingoes and the rare pebble mouse, or take one of the many walks to magnificent waterfalls that truly define the power of nature.

> " Waking up in our safari-style tent at the Karijini Eco Retreat with a warm breeze outside was heaven; it felt so spacious being in the heart of the Pilbara. There was a little path outside our tent that led down to the gorges; our guide Digger took us on this jaw-dropping journey. Standing at the Joffre Gorge Lookout with the red earth and spinifex under our feet, we were transfixed by the enormous rocky escarpments that have been here for billions of years. With the temperature rising into the 30s, we hugged the rim of the gorge and slowly wound our way along the track, mesmerised by the cliff faces in front of us, and the sound of the gushing waterfalls thundering over the rocks.
>
> From a distance, we could hear the sound of people laughing and splashing around in the waters of Fortescue Falls. As we rounded a corner, the falls, an oasis in the middle of the outback, came into view. Everyone was either swimming or lying on the rocks lapping up what Mother Nature had so beautifully created.
>
> It's easy to see why Karijini National Park carries the reputation for being one of the most spectacular parks in Western Australia – it is absolutely beautiful. "

JEN AND CLINT

PLACES WE GO

WHAT TO DO

- Stay at Karijini Eco Retreat, a collaboration between the Department of Parks and Wildlife and the traditional owners of the land, the Banyjima, Kurrama and Innawonga Aboriginal people. Here you have a choice of accommodation from deluxe eco tents through to campsites.
- Stop at Oxer Lookout for a stunning panoramic view over the junction of four incredible gorges, a great introduction to the park.
- Take a dip in any one of the natural swimming holes, such as Fortescue Falls, Fern Pool or Hamersley Gorge.
- Hike into Hancock Gorge with a guide to explore rocky chambers and underground waterways.

KOOKYNIE

Kookynie is the perfect example of what happens when gold is discovered. In 1895, when a group of prospectors got lucky in this area of outback Western Australia, the town was formed almost overnight and was soon thriving with several mines in operation. By 1907, over 3500 people were living here, and the town had a public swimming pool, a racecourse, 11 hotels, seven brass bands, a brewery and electricity. It even had its own red-light district.

Today, the town has just 13 people, and is more or less a living ghost town. From the hundreds of buildings Kookynie boasted in its heyday, now pretty much only the Old Miner's Cottage, Grand Hotel, the Cumberland Street shops and Cosmopolitan Hotel remain to give you a hint as to what this town once looked like.

But the Grand Hotel, still in operation, is more than worth the visit. A quintessential outback pub built in 1902, it serves up a bit of history with its country fare and cold beer, along with many old photographs and memorabilia on display that capture the spirit of the town's former glory.

Kookynie's unique character is its drawcard today, offering a genuine glimpse into the past and how an Australian town can simply appear overnight, and then virtually disappear just as quickly.

> " When we first arrived in this almost-ghost town, we couldn't really make sense of the place. It's like an incredible open-air museum that pays tribute to the gold miners who found their fortunes here. Relics are scattered throughout the streets – an old car that looks like its owner is still coming back, old machinery, parts of buildings, like the old post office.
>
> And when we say parts of buildings, we mean it: apart from the pub and a few houses on the outskirts, there are no other buildings in town, just ruins, essentially. The place doesn't even have a milk bar. Which might all sound a bit dismal, but it's quite the opposite. It's been cleverly done – it doesn't feel like a tourist town – and while the old gold town has a few (a lot!) less people these days, its spirit has remained. Some of the locals, like Judy and Russell, are still making their living from prospecting for gold.
>
> We were invited to meet the locals in the only pub still standing. Of course, like most gold towns, the pub is a place that once was, and still is, the lifeblood of the town. Inside we met the entire town (except for a couple of people who were out of town that night) – and we all fitted into the front bar! Over homemade hamburgers we heard why these locals choose to call this unique place home. The publican Kevin proudly told us how their community is a close-knit one with old values, and how the town is a memorial to those people who went out and did things for the first time. "

JEN AND CLINT

PLACES WE GO

WHAT TO DO

- Visit the Grand Hotel, an iconic Aussie pub that stood through the gold rush and is still operating today.
- Take the walking trail through the remains of the old town, with sites marked out along the way.
- Visit nearby Niagara Dam, an outback oasis with a shady camping area. Constructed in 1897–98, the dam was built to supply nearby mining towns with fresh water, and to water the steam locomotives travelling along the newly constructed railway line to Kookynie.

» The only pub still standing

» Most of the town is in ruins

» View over the lake

» Jen hanging out with a local

» *One of the 'Inside Australia' sculptures on the salt lake*

LAKE BALLARD

Venture into Western Australia's outback and discover a treasure other than the gold the region is so famous for. In the northern Goldfields region near Menzies, Lake Ballard, a salt lake stretching around 70 kilometres from east to west, has become Australia's largest outdoor art gallery. 'Inside Australia', an installation on the lake, consists of 51 life-sized sculptures fixed over 10 square kilometres. Lending an eerie appearance to the flat salt plain and drawing international attention, the work was originally entered into the Perth International Arts Festival and was to be removed afterwards, but interest in the site remained and the statues were left in situ.

The artist, Antony Gormley, chose this location as the canvas for his work for its completely flat and white landscape and virtual 360-degree horizons. Gormley based his sculptures on locals from Menzies, maintaining the life-sized height of the people but reducing their body volume by two-thirds. The resulting artworks are stick-like and rigid, and stand on some of the oldest crusts of earth to be found.

But Lake Ballard is not just a drawcard for tourists wishing to see the installation. It is also one of the rare breeding grounds for the banded stilt, a bird that is so discerning about its nesting ground, it will only choose a recently flooded salt lake. When cyclone Bobby crossed the path of Lake Ballard in 1995, the result was a breeding frenzy when tens of thousands of banded stilts arrived, creating a landmark event in Australia's natural history.

" Camping by the banks of a world-renowned art site would have to go down as one of the more 'unique' places we've slept! What makes the Inside Australia installation so interesting (apart from the obvious visual masterpiece) is the fact that much of the community of Menzies came together to make it, and by a stroke of luck (or genius), they turned their country town into a tourist town!

While we were walking around the lake, we met travellers from all over the world snapping away with their cameras, marvelling at the sculptures. We were lucky enough to be joined by a few locals who featured among the 51 statues; they told us some behind-the-scenes stories about the making of the exhibition. We found out that they had to take all of their clothes off for images to be taken; the images were then used to form the basis of the sculptures. That is how they are all so unique. Now permanent fixtures on the lake, the townspeople commented on how proud they are, and no matter where they are from or what they look like, it united them as one people. One woman told us she liked the fact that her grandchild can visit in the future and know her granny is out there. "

JEN AND CLINT

PLACES WE GO

WHAT TO DO

- Camp at one of the most unique locations in the country, at Lake Ballard's camping area.

- Take your time to properly discover the Inside Australia installation; it can take hours to walk around it properly. It's a photographer's dream and one of the most unique sights you will ever see.

- Scan the skies for birds. A breeding habitat for many species of waterfowl and classified as an Important Bird Area, Lake Ballard is a fantastic birdwatching destination.

MARGARET RIVER

It's where world-class waves meet internationally acclaimed wineries, where spectacular limestone caves lie beneath towering karri forests, and where artisan producers sell gourmet food and boutique beer to a thriving local population of artists and surfers, alongside tourists.

Margaret River is blessed not only with beauty, but also brains. Situated on the south-west coast of Western Australia, its magnificent coastal scenery is underpinned by its passionate community of talented and creative locals. A stay here will most likely encompass sampling award-winning wines, testing out the famous surf breaks, canoeing on the serene Margaret River, tasting cheese, olives, ice-cream and jam created by local producers, and attending a festival or event that the town so capably hosts.

There is no shortage of attractions. Whales pass by between September and December, wildflowers bloom in spring, and the nearby wild Leeuwin-Naturaliste Ridge, which separates the coastline from the hinterland with dramatic rocky scenery, hides one of the best limestone cave systems in Australia.

The Noongar people have had a long and continuing connection with the land around Margaret River, and evidence of their existence here dates back around 48,000 years, with artefacts including animal bones, hearths and human remains uncovered in the Devil's Lair cave, south of Margaret River.

Settlers had to be persuaded to come to the area after World War I before surfers and winemakers put it on the map, but there is no stopping the thousands of visitors who come to enjoy Margaret River today.

" As far as warm welcomes from the locals go, ours in Margaret River was among the best we'd had anywhere. Its relaxed locals include tour guide Sean Blocksidge who runs a local tour company. He not only showed us around, but also kicked off the day with a coffee in a very cool cafe, where he picked up an assortment of delicious goodies produced in the region – Yallingup wood-fired bread and locally grown olives to name just a couple! – ready for our picnic.

Amongst other places, Sean took us to a forest where beautiful spring wildflowers were blooming, and where, he pointed out, Aboriginal people had lived for the best part of 50,000 years. The forest he showed us has an abundance of food, and the honey from the jarrah tree here is regarded as one of the healthiest in the world.

The longer we spent in the region, the more we got the feeling there really must be something special in the soil, for award-winning wineries were everywhere! Over our stay we enjoyed a leisurely afternoon sipping chardonnay at both Fraser Gallop Estate and Leeuwin Estate – we didn't want to leave either!

But it was sitting on the cliff-tops overlooking the expansive ocean that was the highlight of our trip to magical Margaret River. This is the place to come during whale-watching season to spot these majestic creatures offshore. "

JEN AND CLINT

WHAT TO DO

- Head to any of the cellar doors within the Margaret River wine region, including Leeuwin Estate, Cape Mentelle and Vasse Felix, or join a wine tour and be escorted to the best. Many wineries offer sublime dining experiences with views sweeping over the vines to the ocean.

- Explore Mammoth and Lake Caves, two of the magnificent limestone caves in Leeuwin-Naturaliste National Park. Mammoth Cave contains the fossilised remains of prehistoric animals and Lake Cave has an incredible reflective lake.

- Join an eco-friendly canoe or kayak tour on Margaret River.

- Hit any of the local beaches. Whether you want to surf some of the best waves in the country, or look for a more family-friendly swimming beach, the coast has it all.

I find it amazing that grapevines always seem to grow in beautiful parts of the world, and Margaret River is a case in point. Here tall timber forests frame perfectly sculpted beaches. The world's best wine can be sampled with gourmet local produce. And this all comes with a laid-back local attitude that says come, indulge, enjoy.

Chris Horgan, Fremantle, Western Australia

» *Meeting the local winemakers*

» *Margaret River backs onto the expansive Indian Ocean*

» *Award-winning wineries are everywhere in Margaret River*

Mitchell Falls is one of the most remote places in Australia and one of the most exciting to get to, with four-wheel driving and water crossings involved. The helicopter ride over the falls was incredible, as was the view from the top of the cliff overlooking the falls and the gorge. The walk back to camp was fun and involved walking under waterfalls. Swimming in the river near the campground was a fantastic way to end the day.

Sharon Johnstone, Doreen, Victoria

» One of the most inaccessible attractions in the country

» *Jen at a contender for her favourite place in Australia*

MITCHELL FALLS, MITCHELL RIVER NATIONAL PARK

> While writing this book, many people asked us what our favourite place in Australia was. That's a very difficult question to answer, however, the Kimberley's remote Mitchell Plateau would have to be a contender for the number one position. This is really Mother Nature at her finest, and seeing it was one of the highlights of our lives.
>
> We flew over the coastline of the Kimberley to Mitchell Plateau and landed right on the plateau itself. As we trekked through bushland and past waterfalls with locals Joey, Erica and Brownie, Joey shared stories of how his ancestors had lived here for thousands of years, and how this was his backyard growing up. He proudly showed us ancient rock-art sites, many of which have remained untouched for millennia. Among the many different paintings, there were handprints on the rocks. Staring at them was a profound experience that helped us feel connected to the Aboriginal people who had left their imprint here.
>
> Due to the rains, we had to take a helicopter from Big Mertens Falls and landed right in front of Mitchell Falls. To sit there and take it all in was pure magic; there are simply no words to describe it. Our day ended with a swim in the water, which is so pure you can fill your drink bottle. That night, under clear starry skies, Joey broke into song during a scrumptious dinner at Mitchell Falls Wilderness Lodge. It was one of the most unforgettable days we'd ever had.

JEN AND CLINT

PLACES WE GO

Perhaps because they're tucked away in a remote national park in the far north of the Kimberley region, and are accessible only by a rugged four-wheel-drive track or air, Mitchell Falls are relatively unknown – which is all the more reason to visit.

These stunning four-tiered falls are located in Mitchell River National Park, a biologically significant environment rich in breathtaking scenery and rare and extraordinary Aboriginal art. The falls are accessed via a ruggedly beautiful 8.6-kilometre return walking trail over Mitchell Plateau.

A captivating walk, it treats visitors to treasures such as Little Mertens Falls, Aboriginal Gwion (Bradshaw) rock art and Big Mertens Falls, before revealing the jewel in its crown, Mitchell Falls. With four emerald-green pools cascading into one another, surrounded by gorges and iconic red Kimberley rock, they are a powerful sight to behold.

Culturally significant to the local Wunambal people, who believe the falls are one of the Wunggurr (Rainbow) Serpent's main homes, it is important to pay the falls the respect they deserve when visiting.

» Joey and Erica showed Jen some ancient rock-art sites

WHAT TO DO

- Take the walking trail to the falls, visiting the highlights along the way, and enjoy a dip in Mitchell River at the top of the falls when you arrive.
- Book a helicopter transfer back to the carpark, which includes a scenic flight over the falls to view them in all their glory.
- Stay at nearby Mitchell Falls Wilderness Lodge for a stylish and comfortable night in the bush.

NINGALOO REEF

On Australia's west coast, Ningaloo Reef, one of the world's largest fringing reefs, is a superb World Heritage–listed marine park brimming with manta rays, turtles, over 500 species of fish, and hundreds of varieties of colourful coral. Nowhere else in the world can you reach such a large coral reef so effortlessly; indeed, in many places you can access the reef simply by taking a short swim from the beach.

This is a region that's all about its marine life: from humpback whales that pass through on their annual migration between June and November, to rare turtle species that hatch on the beach in January and February, and dugongs that you can watch simply by kayaking out to a more remote spot.

And that's not even the best of it. From April to July every year, Ningaloo Reef welcomes a very special visitor: the incredible whale shark. Visitors at this time of year can experience swimming with a congregation of these superb fish, the largest in the world (they can grow up to 16 metres long).

There's no other experience on earth quite like coming face-to-face with these gentle giants when they gather in this pristine reef environment. It's absolutely exhilarating, a once-in-a-lifetime opportunity that will stay with you forever.

> If I had to list my top 100 adventures in Australia, swimming alongside whale sharks at Ningaloo Reef would be right up there near the top.
>
> From Exmouth, we made our way to the outer reef. A small spotter plane was circling above us looking for the whale sharks and radioing back down to our boat. As soon as one was spotted, there was a flurry of excitement as we all clambered to put our snorkelling gear on. Everyone was pointing to a fin in the water about 100 metres away and before I knew it, we'd all jumped overboard and were bobbing up and down in the water to hopefully catch a glimpse.
>
> 'It's still too far away', I yelled to Clint in a slight panic, worried that I'd miss out. 'Put your head in the water; you're almost on top of it', he yelled back. I put my head down and all of a sudden this giant creature was right before my eyes. I could literally feel my heart thumping out of my chest.
>
> The only way I can describe it is to imagine a high-rise building ploughing through the water. My initial nerves were quickly replaced with an overwhelming sense of calm, as this gentle giant made its way through the water, not bothered in the slightest by us all angling for a glimpse. It felt like time stood still … and then as quickly as it had appeared, it disappeared deep into the ocean.
>
> It was one of the most humbling things we've ever had the privilege of experiencing.

JEN AND CLINT

PLACES WE GO

WHAT TO DO

- Book a tour with an operator from Coral Bay or Exmouth to experience swimming with the whale sharks (between April and July).
- Meet another large visitor, the humpback whale, between June and November, when whale-watching tours are available.
- Snorkel straight off many of the beaches in the region, with schools of clownfish and coral just metres from the sand.

» Ready to jump back in the water for a whale shark encounter!

Manta rays, whale sharks, loggerhead turtles, dugongs, whales and beautiful corals: these are just a few of the things we saw at Ningaloo Reef while diving and snorkelling. Along with the local produce, beautiful beaches and friendly locals, it is like another Great Barrier Reef, only more mysterious and so exciting. There's no better Aussie place to get your full wildlife experience!

Grace Swain, Glebe, New South Wales

» *Snorkel with the gentle giants of the ocean*

» Enjoy a drink at Cottlesloe

» *Perth is all about the outdoors lifestyle (and who wouldn't be, with weather like this?)*

PERTH

One of the most remote cities in the world, Perth is a vibrant and energetic hub built around the shores of the Swan River. Occupying a beautiful stretch of the Indian Ocean coastline, its sunny climate affords its residents and visitors plenty of time outdoors, enjoying its world-class beaches, parklands, festivals and sunsets.

The city's locals are friendly and relaxed, and it's sometimes described as a big country town. Yet Perth still has its finger on the pulse, and rivals the best when it comes to culture, the arts, dining and commerce. And there is always an escape: within a very short period of time you can be relaxing on the surrounding waterways, or even enjoying secluded bays on tranquil Rottnest Island (*see* p. 127).

Originally founded by Captain James Stirling in 1829, it was vested as a city in 1856 and named for Perth in Scotland. Its population swelled during the gold rushes in the late 19th century, and has experienced another surge in the last two decades thanks to mining booms. Today it is Australia's fourth largest capital.

Perth's port town of Fremantle is a historic precinct that's always buzzing with festivity. Markets, street artists, boutique shops, and cafes and bars all share the precinct's heritage-listed streets, and you can always be guaranteed a lively atmosphere.

" There is so much to love about Perth, and we've spent a lot of time there. Its expansive coastline and meandering river make for a truly beautiful city where you can easily be swept away by the outdoor lifestyle that its residents enjoy. On any given weekend you'll find people out exploring their backyard – whether it's a jog along the Swan River, a barbecue in the park, a day out at one of the city's many beautiful white-sand beaches, or an outdoor 'Sunday session' at the pub.

One of our favourite places is Cottesloe Beach, where we've enjoyed many a day splashing around in the water, followed by afternoon drinks and dinner at the superb Indiana bar and restaurant, perched prettily right on the beach. Watching a famous Western Australian sunset over the Indian Ocean from this idyllic vantage point makes for some very happy memories indeed. "

JEN AND CLINT

PLACES WE GO

Kings Park is a truly unique and special place to visit. There is no other city in the world that offers such a vast tract of natural bushland right in the heart of the city. It's filled year-round with an abundance of natural flora and fauna, and has priceless views of the city and meandering Swan River at every turn.

Benjamin Croker, Dianella, Western Australia

WHAT TO DO

- Grab a towel and head to Cottesloe Beach for a swim and snorkel, or join the surfers at Scarborough.
- Take a cruise along the Swan River and travel from the skyscrapers of the CBD, past wealthy neighbourhoods and parklands, and end up in Fremantle.
- Spend some time in Kings Park, one of the largest inner-city parks in the world and the most popular visitor destination in Western Australia. Here you can discover Perth's Indigenous history on a guided walk, catch panoramic views over the Swan River and Darling Range, or visit the State War Memorial.

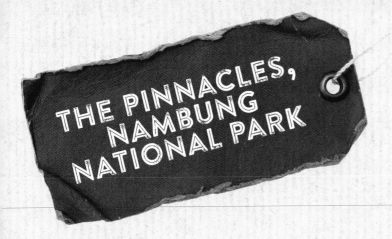

THE PINNACLES, NAMBUNG NATIONAL PARK

» *Some of the spires are several metres tall*

An eerie desert landscape greets you in Western Australia's Nambung National Park on the Coral Coast. In contrast to the neighbouring sparkling Indian Ocean, the yellow dunes of the desert are host to thousands of rock spires known as the Pinnacles. Some of these spires are several metres high and they rise out of the sand to resemble something that wouldn't look out of place on Mars.

Thought to have begun forming around 80,000 years ago, the spires are the product of a geological process that cemented layers of limestone beneath the sand. In periods of drier weather, the sand was stripped away leaving the Pinnacles exposed.

They're best viewed at sunrise and sunset, when the changing light creates incredible colours, shadows and patterns over the landscape. The starkness of the spires against the desert and sky makes for a unique and unforgettable panorama.

Emus, kangaroos, birds and other wildlife can be found between the spires in the early and late parts of the day. Take the walking trail and marvel at how the Pinnacles only really became known to European Australians in the 1960s.

This is an amazing place to visit; it's like walking on another planet. I'd never seen anything like it before. The sun at sunset lights the fantastic formations up so they are much more distinct and photogenic, and there are no crowds at this time of day, as the bus tours have gone home. It's definitely the best time of day to visit to see the Pinnacles at their finest.

**Lorraine Pearce,
Frenchville, Queensland**

WHAT TO DO

- Take the scenic walk or drive on a trail that winds past the ancient pillars.
- Visit the interpretive discovery centre to learn how the Pinnacles formed and more about the region's biodiversity.

» *Rotto: 19 kilometres off the coast of Perth, but a world away*

ROTTNEST ISLAND

A world away from the city of Perth (*see* p. 123), yet just 19 kilometres off its coast, Rottnest Island is home to secluded bays, dazzling beaches, rich history and unique wildlife that will both surprise and amaze you.

From the moment you arrive on 'Rotto' by ferry, you are immersed in a laid-back atmosphere that defines your time here. Feel complete freedom as you snorkel crystal-clear waters. Explore the island's walking trails discovering rich Indigenous and colonial history along the way. Climb the Wadjemup Lighthouse for breathtaking views. And encounter wildlife, such as whales on their annual migration and the island's native resident, the quokka.

With virtually no cars on the island, the main options here are bike and foot. Breathe in the fresh ocean air and enjoy the peace as you set your own pace. There are over 63 beaches and 20 bays to be enjoyed in whichever way you please, be it swimming, surfing, snorkelling or kayaking.

The island's first inhabitants, the Noongar people, occupied Rottnest when it was still attached to the mainland around 7000 years ago. Rising sea levels separated the two, and the name 'Wadjemup', meaning 'place across the water', was given to the island by the traditional owners. European exploration began in the 17th century, and when Dutch captain Willem de Vlamingh spent six days on the island in 1696, he named it 'Rotte Nest', literally meaning 'rats' nest', after mistaking the island's native marsupials, the quokka, for rats.

Today the quokka is a natural drawcard for Rottnest, which is one of only a few areas in the world where this marsupial resides, largely because the island's isolation means it is free from predators.

» *Once mistaken for rats, quokkas are much cuter!*

WHAT TO DO

- Tackle the 9.4-kilometre Rottnest Island Wadjemup Walk Trail to discover the island's environmental and cultural values, as well as its spectacular beauty.
- Take a scenic flight over the island for a bird's-eye view of its stark beauty.
- Follow one of the snorkel trails to discover the island's coral reefs and fish.

SHARK BAY

On the far west coast of Australia, in an area of pristine wilderness, some very special visitors have been coming close to shore for more than forty years. But the bottlenose dolphins of Monkey Mia are just one of the unique reasons to visit Shark Bay, a World Heritage–listed area of more than 2.2 million hectares covering two bays and side-by-side peninsulas.

It's known to the area's original Indigenous inhabitants, the local Malgana people, as Gathaagudu, meaning 'two waters'. Europeans came to the region initially for pearling. In the 1960s, a local fisherman began feeding the bottlenose dolphins and news spread quickly, creating the influx of visitors that exists today.

The Monkey Mia dolphins might be the most famous attraction here, visiting daily to interact with visitors, but other treasures include the dugongs, manta rays and turtles of Shark Bay Marine Park; white sandy beaches bordered by red cliffs and turquoise waters; the ancient stromatolites of Hamelin Pool, the largest and oldest living fossils on earth; and Shell Beach, formed from billions of tiny shells and one of only a few places in the world where shells replace sand in this way.

With more than 1500 kilometres of shoreline framing a spectacular marine park environment, there are unique natural wonders to be found around every corner in Shark Bay.

WHAT TO DO

- Get a deeper understanding of the area at the Shark Bay World Heritage Discovery Centre, detailing all aspects of the area from its history through to its World Heritage listing.
- Take an Indigenous walking tour to learn secrets of local bush tucker and bush medicine with the traditional owners of the land.
- Take a four-wheel-drive tour through Francois Peron National Park, one of Australia's most significant natural wilderness areas and home to many rare and endangered species.
- Meet the bottlenose dolphins during their daily visit to the shores of Monkey Mia.

Beaches covered in the whitest sand I've ever seen, crystal-clear water, phenomenal snorkelling spots, wonderful people, witnessing the beauty of free and beautiful dolphins ... what more could you want?! This is an amazing experience that I hope to have again one day.

Jessica Jackson, Melbourne, Victoria

» *Feeding time*

NORTHERN TERRITORY

» The timeless Ellery Creek Big Hole

» Jen and Clint can't keep the smiles off their faces in the Red Centre

I don't think you've seen Australia until you've seen the West Macs. They have the ability to entice and amaze beyond belief. From the richness of the morning sun on red rock to the harsh heat of the day, the ranges are mysterious and intriguing. There is a calm and magical feeling when you're here that is almost medicinal. There's something for people of all fitness levels, beautiful scenic drives, casual and challenging walks, four-wheel-drive tracks and secluded camping locations.

**Cassy Mciver, Kambah,
Australian Capital Territory**

» A town nestled in a desert that seems to go on forever

ALICE SPRINGS & MACDONNELL RANGES

Sitting smack bang in the middle of the desert, Alice Springs is the heart of Australia and the gateway to all the Red Centre has to offer. It is one of the country's best Aboriginal art centres, and boasts incredible galleries and opportunities to meet the artists. A growing cafe culture is also emerging, so you have your choice of places to sit back and enjoy a latte.

The East and West MacDonnell Ranges spread out hundreds of kilometres either side of Alice Springs, rising up from the floor of the desert. Home to the highest mountains in the Northern Territory, including Mount Zeil at 1531 metres, the 644-kilometre-long range is the product of 350 million years of sculpture by the elements, and is one of the oldest regions in the world.

The 'West Macs' start just minutes from Alice Springs; here you can enjoy a permanent waterhole and rock wallabies at Simpsons Gap. Further west, watch the sun light up the red rock at Standley Chasm at midday or set over Mount Sonder from Glen Helen Gorge at dusk.

The 'East Macs' are home to some of the Eastern Arrernte Aboriginal people's stories, with large rock paintings at Emily and Jessie Gaps, and over 6000 prehistoric rock carvings, plus art sites at N'Dhala Gorge. Arltunga Historical Reserve is an eerie ghost town that was the site of a 1930s gold rush, and, intersecting the East Macs, Trephina Gorge is blessed with a sandy creek bed, quartzite cliffs and river red gums.

" Alice is a place dear to our hearts. Whether we've driven or flown there, both modes of transport have given us an appreciation for just how remote Alice is within that immense red desert that seems to go on forever.

The Aboriginal art capital of Australia, the town is full of art galleries overflowing with intricate paintings of stories handed down for thousands of years. You're surrounded by art in this region, from the rock art just 10 minutes from town to the locals painting under the shade of a gum tree in the city centre.

One of my favourite memories is from when we took the drive along Red Centre Way (towards Uluru). There are so many gaps and gorges we were spoilt for choice, but we decided to stop off at Ellery Creek Big Hole for a picnic and a swim. I remember floating in the water looking up at the timeless landscape, and felt transported back millions of years.

We then stopped off at Glen Helen Resort – an old cattle station that's turned its hand to tourism – for the night and we met up with travellers from all over the world, many in the middle of travelling right around Australia. We were all there admiring this truly unique part of the world. Over a scrumptious dinner, everyone was commenting on how privileged they felt to be in the amazing outback. "

JEN AND CLINT

PLACES WE GO

WHAT TO DO

- Hike part or all of the 223-kilometre Larapinta Trail, one of Australia's best bushwalking experiences on the high-ridge line of the West MacDonnell Ranges.
- Drive between Alice Springs and Glen Helen Gorge on a day trip, taking in Simpsons Gap, Standley Chasm, Ellery Creek Big Hole and Ormiston Gorge on the way, and finishing with an evening at Glen Helen Resort.
- See the sun rise over the MacDonnell Ranges on a hot-air balloon ride, one of the best ways to begin your time in 'the Alice'. With a bit of luck you'll glide over a mob of red kangaroos, the perfect introduction to life in the Red Centre.
- Visit the Aboriginal art galleries in Todd Mall to appreciate the work and stories of the local Arrernte people, who have lived here for over 20,000 years.
- Discover the Alice Springs Desert Park, where, in just a few hours, you can discover the secrets of the central Australian deserts, including hundreds of plant and animal species.

DARWIN

The heat, the humidity, the thunderstorms, the monsoon, the people, the culture, the lifestyle, the bush. It is in Australia, yes, but so remotely different to the Australia most people know – and yet, it's more Australian than the Australia most people are used to. The vastness surrounding this modern tropical paradise and its accessibility to natural gems such as Kakadu, Adelaide River and the immense interior add to its appeal, which cannot be described until you experience it yourself. Darwin and the Top End? Tops. End of.

Andre Dalton, Hepburn, Victoria

The tropical capital of the Northern Territory, Darwin is more than just a gateway to the wonders of the Top End. Spend a few days here and soak up the balmy and relaxed atmosphere, and melting pot of cultures, where everyone is welcome.

The city has been almost entirely rebuilt twice, once because of a Japanese air raid on 19 February 1942, when 188 warplanes attacked Darwin during World War II. The bombs killed at least 243 people and destroyed much of the city in what was the largest wartime attack on Australian soil.

The second tragedy came on Christmas Day 1974 when cyclone Tracy struck, killing 71 people and devastating over 70 per cent of the city's buildings in one of Australia's worst natural disasters.

Today, Darwin is a modern city with a rich history and it boasts a vibrant waterfront precinct, buzzing with cafes, bars and restaurants. Mindil Beach Sunset Market comes alive on Thursday and Sunday evenings between May and October. This is when people descend on the beachfront with picnic blankets, chairs and tables to sample some of the multicultural cuisine the market is famous for, while simultaneously watching the sun dip into the sea.

» *The city comes to life at the sunset market*

" Strolling through the sunset market at Mindil Beach gives a great insight into the multicultural city of Darwin, because the market is a celebration of all those who call this place home. It's filled with food stalls from all over the world that fuse seamlessly together, with everyone enjoying the positive vibe. When we were there, the sky was a flaming orange, musicians were drawing a crowd, and children were dancing on the grass under the shade of trees.

A pretty-looking city that sits on the aqua-coloured Indian Ocean, Darwin is a fascinating place to explore. Steeped in World War II history, we followed a well-made bike track to check out some of the historic sites, such as the War Memorial down by the esplanade. Standing there we thought about those who had lost their lives during the Japanese air raid, and also about all of our diggers who fight for the freedoms we enjoy today. "

JEN AND CLINT

`PLACES WE GO` ➤

WHAT TO DO

- Take a sailing trip on Darwin Harbour at sunset, watching the city light up from the water and the stars appear above you on a balmy evening.
- Discover some of the country's most prolific Indigenous artists at any of the city's art centres or galleries.
- Join the locals at Darwin's iconic markets. From the Mindil Beach Sunset Market to Parap Village Markets on a Saturday, your senses will be saturated by the range of cuisines and arts and crafts on offer.
- Don't miss the open-air Deckchair Cinema on Darwin Harbour, which shows old classics and new films under the stars in the dry season.

» The red, red dirt

» All aboard!

THE GHAN

This is one of the greatest train journeys in the world. Connecting Adelaide in the south and Darwin in the north, the epic *Ghan* journey has been traversing some of the most beautiful and rugged landscapes in Australia since 1929, and offers one of the most exciting explorations of the country's inhospitable interior.

As soon as the *Ghan* picks up speed out of Adelaide, and the rolling plains begin to give way to the Flinders Ranges, you truly feel like you're following in the footsteps of Afghan cameleers who pioneered this route 150 years ago. Over three days, the train journey reveals panoramic landscapes best enjoyed from the comfort of your train seat. Watch as nature puts on its top performance as you travel through the heart of Australia; you might be treated to a mob of wild kangaroos crossing the desert or a spectacular Red Centre sunset.

On board, choose between red service with day/night lounge chairs, gold service with twin or single sleeper cabins, or platinum service, a luxurious experience with deluxe accommodation, double beds, ensuite and room service. Gold and platinum guests share a cosy club-like lounge and an elegant restaurant-car where the experience is shared with new friends.

The *Ghan* makes stops so you can experience the iconic locations in its path. The oasis of Alice Springs (*see* p. 133) is more than just a gateway to the other remarkable trophies of the outback; it's a cultural mecca in its own right. Then the ochre earth eventually transitions to the tropical north, where a stop in Katherine to experience its revered gorge (*see* p. 144) is a must. The transcontinental journey comes to its conclusion in Darwin, where Top End adventures await.

The most memorable trip I have ever experienced was travelling north from Adelaide to Darwin on the *Ghan*. Every Australian should take this inspiring trip during their lifetime, seeing places like Alice Springs, Katherine and Darwin (*see* p. 134) along the way. Must-sees from Alice Springs are Kings Canyon (*see* p. 146), Uluṟu (*see* p. 157) and Kata Tjuṯa (*see* p. 142), which are all majestic. These are places you can visit many times and always be in awe.

Glenda Grigg, Melbourne, Victoria

WHAT TO DO

- Make the most of off-train excursions along the way to experience the best of this incredible country. Join an Alice Springs Explorer tour to discover the town's history, or visit the renowned Alice Springs Desert Park to bring to life the vistas you've been enjoying out of the train window.

- Cruise through Katherine Gorge and take to the skies in a helicopter to truly experience the landscape from above. (Note: off-train excursions are not included with every package and might incur additional costs.)

KAKADU NATIONAL PARK

It is hard to get your head around the scale of Kakadu National Park. Set in the tropical Top End, and an easy three-hour drive from Darwin, it is one of the most significant environments in the country and a cultural treasure.

Australia's biggest national park at 20,000 square kilometres, World Heritage–listed Kakadu is home to one-third of all bird species found in the country. Spectacular wetlands and waterholes attract bird species by the hundreds – all flocking to congregate amongst the floodwaters and lush plant life – along with other wildlife, including kangaroos, buffalo, dingoes and crocodiles.

On land, the culture and spirit of the Bininj/Mungguy, Kakadu's traditional owners and one of the oldest living societies in the world, is brought to life. The Ubirr and Nourlangie art sites are just two examples where ancient rock-art galleries some dating back to 20,000 years, share stories of land and culture, and stir many emotions in connection with Australia's first peoples.

Well protected and conserved under a joint management scheme between the traditional owners and Parks Australia, this environment is nature at its best, with breathtaking waterfalls over gorges rich in colour and landscape, sunrises reflected in pools of gold on still billabongs, and brolgas dancing at the edge of flood plains. From some vantage points in the park you can capture expansive views over rivers, billabongs and lowlands, home to rare and endemic plants and animals.

Every part of this land is an adventure, an experience and an education to be enjoyed by everyone, and shared and protected for generations to come.

> Kakadu is a place that we think everyone in Australia needs to experience. To explore the Aboriginal rock-art sites is quite overwhelming when you consider that the drawings represent one of the longest historical records of any group of people in the world. We joined a tour of one of the most significant sites, Nourlangie, on which our guide Doug passionately brought ancient stories to life. Sitting together at the lookout over Anbangang Billabong, we were treated to the most magnificent sunset, casting a brilliant glow on the rock and surrounding plains.
>
> Lapping up every moment of the 'magic hour' here in the Top End, we were up early the following day for a sunrise cruise on Yellow Water Billabong, Kakadu's most famous wetland. As we drifted out onto the water, with only the sounds of the local birdlife and insects for company, the sun revealed itself at the bottom of the sky. It lit up the entire flood plain with a golden glow unlike anything we had ever seen before. With barely a ripple on the water, a massive saltwater crocodile suddenly appeared alongside our boat, as if saying hello and allowing us to witness its magnificent prehistoric body.
>
> Around every turn in this ancient land there is another surprise. We ended our Kakadu adventure at Maguk Gorge surrounded by the gushing sounds of the waterfalls. This timeless landscape really is a national treasure that should always be protected by us all.

JEN AND CLINT

PLACES WE GO

WHAT TO DO

- Visit the Ubirr and Nourlangie rock-art sites for fascinating art that represents one of the longest historical records of any group of people in the world.
- Join a Yellow Water Billabong cruise at sunrise or sunset to watch the flood plains come alive with birds and animals at these magical times of the day.
- Make your way to one of the park's majestic waterfalls, such as Gunlom Falls, Twin Falls or Jim Jim Falls, to marvel at these natural spectacles. Swim at your own risk!
- Visit the Mamukala Wetlands in the dry season to watch them come to life with thousands of migratory magpie geese.

There's something about Kakadu that feels arrestingly surreal. It's like journeying through time, away from the fast-paced life into an ancient world filled with history and natural wonder. Cruising along breathtaking billabongs, surrounded by unique flora and fauna, amidst thundering waterfalls: what a sight to behold! Touring around majestic Aboriginal rock art, filled with the most beautiful galleries of cave paintings depicting stories of Dreamtime: simply, indescribably marvellous.

**Melly Legiman,
Mount Waverley, Victoria**

» *Picture-perfect Kakadu*

I loved wandering around Karlu Karlu/ Devils Marbles. I walked around and over the 'marbles' and felt like I was in a natural playground ... I tried to imagine what the Dreamtime story would be to explain these very big boulders, balancing askew on top of each other, each different from the other, some splitting over time, all awesome. In this ordered world we live in, it was so wonderful to just 'be' amongst such a naturally random landscape.

Sue Flockart, Sandringham, Victoria

» *Catch the rocks glowing red–gold at sunrise and sunset*

» *There are hundreds more rocks than you'd expect to see at Karlu Karlu*

KARLU KARLU / DEVILS MARBLES

Known as Karlu Karlu to the local Warumungu, Kaytetye, Alyawarra and Warlpiri Aboriginal people, the Devils Marbles are granite boulders that are scattered across a desert landscape of spinifex and acacia like giant marbles. Some of them, precariously balanced on top of each other, seem to defy gravity.

Formed over millions of years through the erosion of a single block of stone, these unique formations south of Tennant Creek in the Northern Territory are still cracking and changing, creating an evolving landscape. While Karlu Karlu means 'round boulders' to the traditional owners, the site was also named the Devils Marbles in 1870 when John Ross, an explorer on the Australian Overland Telegraph Line expedition exclaimed: 'This is the devil's country. He's even emptied his bag of marbles around the place'.

There are more boulders to see than just the two pictured in so many images. Hundreds, reaching up to six metres in height, stretch as far as the eye can see on either side of the Sturt Highway. Several self-guided walks take you up close to the geological masterpieces, which are all different and unique, and interpretive signage explains how they were formed and some of the Aboriginal mythology surrounding them. Most of the reserve is a registered sacred site, and many stories and traditions are associated with this magical area.

> While it feels like the Australian desert goes on forever when driving across it, there are so many intriguing stops along the way, and Karlu Karlu is one of them. Right out in the middle of Australia's unforgiving, flat desert, the giant boulders seem to magically appear out of nowhere.
>
> This was one of those special places where we felt compelled to put down the camera. We spent the entire afternoon exploring the ancient formations, wondering how on earth they got there. Playing a simple game of hide-and-seek turned into a memorable afternoon, and we wondered who else had done the same over the past millennia.
>
> Travelling through the entire Red Centre, we were on our way to Uluru, and the Devils Marbles made for a fascinating entrance into a region that's filled with rich Aboriginal mythological stories.

JEN AND CLINT

PLACES WE GO

» A special place where Jen and Clint felt compelled to put down the camera (well, for most of the time)

WHAT TO DO

- Stay overnight in the adjoining bush campground to see the boulders bathed in the golden-red light of sunset and sunrise.
- Take one of the informal self-guided walks and shoot endless photos of the balancing and splitting rocks.
- Stop at Tennant Creek, 105 kilometres north of Karlu Karlu, famous for its gold-rush history and cattle-grazing country.

KATA TJUṮA

On the desert road to Kata Tjuṯa in Australia's Red Centre, you can't help but feel a sense of awe as the enormous, red rocky domes start to come into view, spread panoramically across the horizon. All shapes and sizes, but all towering over the desert landscape, the 36 domes that make up the formation are spread over an area of more than 20 kilometres, and are a sacred Aboriginal site within the Uluṟu–Kata Tjuṯa National Park.

The traditional owners are the Anangu people, who have inhabited this land for more than 22,000 years, a mere speck in the lifespan of the rocks, which are said to have been formed 500 million years ago.

Walking through the domes, the trail twists and turns around the spectacular monoliths, some of which hover over 500 metres above the plain. The landscape is rocky and undulating, and it's hard to stop yourself from constantly craning your neck to see the tops of the rocks dominating the sky above you.

Throughout the land, there's an overarching sense of spirituality. The legends associated with Kata Tjuṯa that the traditional owners choose to share remain at the top of your mind as you explore the rocks they hold so sacred. It is a privilege to visit this landmark and experience the culture and heritage of such an important site.

We saw Kata Tjuṯa, or the Olgas as they're also known, on our very first visit to the Northern Territory. It's hard to describe the feeling of this place – to be walking through a sacred Aboriginal site was humbling, and then to add such an imposing, beautifully carved landscape pretty much silenced us all.

We got up in the dark, and made our way out to the site to see the colour of the rocks as the sun rose; there was barely a word muttered amongst us as we waited. As soon as the first light hit the domes, they glowed a deep orange; it was like watching a show for that magic hour to mark the beginning of the day. Realising this has been happening for around 500 million years was beyond staggering.

As day broke, the sky was a deep blue, the perfect backdrop to show off the unique formations. Wandering through them, I kept asking our guide if he could tell us some Aboriginal stories about the place, but he'd only reply: 'Not even I know, and I have been working here for over a decade.' Marvelling that Aboriginal people had lived in the area for over 22,000 years, we walked in silence, overcome by such beauty that will hopefully still be here long after we are all gone.

JEN AND CLINT

PLACES WE GO

WHAT TO DO

- Take one of the walking trails through the domes, ranging from short and easy, to longer and more challenging.
- Witness Kata Tjuṯa from the viewing platforms at sunrise or sunset, and watch the domes glow and vary in colour in the changing light.

» Overcome by the beauty of Kata Tjuṯa

A few years ago, I travelled from Alice Springs to Darwin on the *Ghan* (*see* p. 136). We stopped along the way at Katherine and took a Katherine Gorge river cruise. The sunshine was glorious, the water pristine and the massive rock formations on both sides made me realise I was a mere dot in the grand scheme of things. I felt like the only person on earth and completely in awe. It's the most tranquil place I have ever been and an amazing experience, a must-do!

Alison Brennan, Kialla, Victoria

» *The best way to see rock-art sites is with a local guide*

» *There's nothing like a dip in one of the swimming holes (but make sure there are no crocs first!)*

KATHERINE GORGE (NITMILUK) NATIONAL PARK

» Katherine Gorge is thiiiiiiisssss big

Whether you're exploring it by foot, boat, helicopter or kayak, Katherine Gorge is a powerful reminder of the forces of nature. The Katherine River, flowing from Arnhem Land, forged a series of 13 gorges through ancient sandstone to create this natural wonder. The stories of the national park come alive amid its towering escarpments, idyllic waterways, cascading waterfalls, caves, beaches and Aboriginal rock-art sites.

The area is the traditional land of the Jawoyn and Dagomen Aboriginal people, whose rock art depicted in caves and shelters throughout the park tells of their culture and heritage. In 1989 Katherine Gorge was handed back to the Jawoyn people who established Nitmiluk National Park in joint management with the Parks and Wildlife Commission of the Northern Territory; their ancient history is shared at the park's visitor information centre.

One of the best ways to experience the park is to canoe the length of the first three gorges, taking in the diversity of landscapes, discovering ancient Jawoyn rock paintings and going for a dip in the refreshing waters. This intimate adventure on the Katherine River's serene waters is not only a glimpse into the natural habitat of the resident wildlife, but a spiritual experience connecting with the history and people of the land.

> " Our boat ride on Katherine Gorge was jaw-droppingly beautiful – it really is a sight to see. As we cruised upstream, dwarfed by the timeless, dramatic, rocky escarpments, we passed markers that showed how high the waters rise here during the wet season.
>
> Our guide Gary was a local Aboriginal man who took great pride in sharing the stories of his ancestors in this region. After a 20-minute boat ride we entered an area that was filled with elaborate Aboriginal rock art dating back thousands of years. We got out of the boat and walked around, admiring the incredible art. Gary said: 'I feel like they [his ancestors] left these stories here for us to talk about and keep our culture alive'. He told us he took great comfort in seeing these paintings and often wondered how it would have been living here thousands of years ago.
>
> Just when we thought our afternoon couldn't get any more memorable, Gary performed a brolga dance for us, a traditional dance associated with this large waterbird. We felt incredibly privileged to be here with Gary as he not only shared his culture, but the history of our beautiful country. "

JEN AND CLINT

PLACES WE GO

WHAT TO DO

- Cruise through Katherine Gorge, an essential experience, especially if you have limited time. Cruises depart frequently, but are subject to weather and seasonal conditions; you have the option of visiting two or three of the gorges, and can also cruise at sunrise or sunset.
- Take an overnight canoe tour, paddling away from the crowds as far as the sixth gorge and camping overnight under the stars for a truly authentic experience.
- Go for a refreshing dip in one of the delightful swimming holes in the park (but check with rangers first to make sure it's safe in relation to crocodiles).
- Explore one of the excellent walking trails, anything from a short 300-metre stroll to a 65-kilometre five-day trek.

KINGS CANYON

Halfway between Uluru and Alice Springs in Australia's Red Centre lies a perfect excuse for a stopover: Kings Canyon. Located in Watarrka National Park, this ancient formation of gorges, waterholes and vertical sandstone walls rising up to 100 metres is hundreds of millions of years in the making.

The canyon can be explored on the 6-kilometre rim walk, which has some challenging climbs and rocky landscape underfoot. Those that venture on this walk are rewarded with spectacular gorge views, dense with red rock and soaring cliffs above palm forests and other lush plant life, such as that found in the ancient Garden of Eden. A less challenging option is the Kings Canyon floor walk, where the gorge can be viewed from the ground below.

To appreciate the canyon in its full beauty against the backdrop of the harsh Australian desert, take a scenic flight over it. From the air, the full scale of the landscape reveals itself, and the red rocky domes and cliffs juxtapose with both the abundant plants they shelter and the big, blue desert sky above.

> " Kings Canyon deserves its regal name. It's simply stunning. You can see why, back in 1872, an Englishman by the name of Giles called it 'an agreeable creek', for it's certainly that, and then some!
>
> Our time here was actually quite overwhelming for many of the people in our group. We had been travelling together around the region for a few days, and really didn't know how incredible Kings Canyon would be. Uluru gets so much of the attention, and yet when we took the 6-kilometre canyon rim walk, it totally blew us away. The sheer magnitude of the place is striking; you feel like a mere speck in the big picture. We had a moment when we sat down and just took it all in, trying to find the words to sum up how we felt. But ultimately, our silence said it all.
>
> Inspired by the dramatic landscape, that night we sat around the campfire together at nearby Kings Creek Station, sharing stories about what it means to be Australian. This place left a huge impact on all of us. "

JEN AND CLINT

PLACES WE GO

Nothing could be more different from the hustle and bustle of city life than gazing at the magical beauty of Kings Canyon, strolling around the canyon rim or flying over the canyon at sunset. The calls of dingoes at night and the circling eagles are a reminder of the wildlife that surrounds you in this remote corner of the Northern Territory, and if you're lucky you will get to see the waterfalls created by a downpour over the Watarrka National Park.

Melissa Zini, Mooroopna, Victoria

WHAT TO DO

- Stay on nearby Kings Creek Station for an authentic outback cattle-station experience and an opportunity to explore the land by camel or quad bike.
- Take either of the two walks on offer at Kings Canyon. Go early in the day or later in the afternoon to avoid the heat in the middle of the day.

» Walk around the rim or fly over the canyon

» Kings Canyon totally blew Jen and Clint away

» The epic termite mounds

» *Cool down at one of the natural spring-fed swimming holes*

LITCHFIELD NATIONAL PARK

Walk through a rainforest that comes alive with every step, jump off waterfalls into beautiful fresh cold water, swim out to the middle of a swimming hole to sit and ponder on ancient rocks, follow hiking trails that make you feel like you were the first person to discover them.

Rebecca Ford, Crestmead, Queensland

Just one and a half hours from Darwin, 1500-square-kilometre Litchfield National Park is an easy escape from the city and a welcome respite from the Top End heat. With its spectacular waterfalls that thunder over a plateau, and natural spring-fed swimming holes, it's the perfect place to cool down.

It's also well known for its giant magnetic termite mounds, incredible natural architectural structures built by and housing thousands of termites. These remarkable mounds have a perfect north–south orientation to minimise sun exposure and thus protect the termites, which are vulnerable to temperature change. They're truly a sight to behold, resembling a graveyard with thousands of headstones.

Rich in flora and fauna, this area is also a haven for bushwalkers and four-wheel drivers, with lush monsoon rainforest, eucalypt woodland and numerous waterholes, perfect for a dip.

Home to Aboriginal people for thousands of years, and encompassing the traditional lands of the Koongurrukun, Marranunggu, Werat and Waray clans, the park was named after the explorer Frederick Litchfield who was the first European to discover the area in 1864. Until the 1950s it was used for tin and copper mining and then logging, and continued as pastoral land until 1985 when it was declared a national park. Today it's flourishing with the conservation of its flora and fauna, as well as its rich Indigenous history.

" As soon as we arrived at Litchfield National Park, our entire *Places We Go* filming family threw on their bathers and jumped straight into the crystal-clear swimming holes. The water was cool enough to give relief from the unrelenting heat of the Northern Territory, and warm enough to want to splash about in all day, making for the perfect Sunday afternoon picnic destination. You could swim under the gushing waterfalls or in the calm of the rockpools, and the park was filled with people soaking up this gift from Mother Nature.

As the afternoon kicked on, we enjoyed one of those leisurely picnics that you never want to end and were joined by local Indigenous guide Natasha and her two young children. Natasha said Litchfield holds fond memories for her, because not only were her ancestors from here, but this was her playground growing up and is her favourite place to bring her family. She said with the watering holes so close together, and being so close to Darwin, this is where all the locals, and travellers too, love to come and soak up the spectacular surrounds. "

JEN AND CLINT

PLACES WE GO

WHAT TO DO

- Swim beneath spectacular waterfalls in the rockpools of Florence and Wangi Falls, safe from crocodiles in the dry season.
- Visit Blyth Homestead, established in 1928 as an outstation and a typical example of the tough conditions faced by pioneers on pastoral leases. It has some well-preserved remnants of pastoral and mining times.
- Walk or four-wheel drive to the Lost City, a formation of sandstone blocks and pillars that have been shaped over time and look like some long-forgotten civilisation.

MARY RIVER NATIONAL PARK

» *Clint keeps an eye out for crocs at Mary River*

On the road between Darwin and Kakadu, you'd be forgiven for passing through Mary River National Park without even realising you had. Its treasures lie hidden on either side of the Arnhem Highway, but it's truly deserving of a few days of your time.

On a wetlands cruise of Corroboree Billabong, the rising sun lifts the fog from the floodplains to reveal a wonderland of birds in their natural environment. Jabiru fossick among pink waterlilies, and are joined by ibis, brolga, egrets, herons, sea eagles, magpie geese and more. Beneath them, the beady eyes of crocodiles lurk lazily just above the water (don't worry: the crocs are more interested in basking in the sun than anything else ...). If you're feeling lucky, throw in a line and try to catch the elusive trophy of the Top End, the barramundi.

As the day warms up, take a guided wilderness cruise of Mary River, which will reveal a tranquil and beautiful river system home to twice as many saltwater crocodiles as any other river in the world. This is a peaceful journey without the crowds of Kakadu.

It's just as easy to find adventure off the water, with creek crossings, giant termite mounds and pristine billabongs along Hardies 4WD Track showcasing the incredible Northern Territory outback in all its glory.

66 To head out on a river that is home to more crocodiles than any other river in the world is pretty daunting and intriguing at the same time. We certainly had our hearts in our mouths. But after seeing our first saltie [saltwater croc], we felt more relaxed and enjoyed a thrilling afternoon witnessing these prehistoric creatures in their natural habitat.

From the safety of our boat, we made our way up the river literally spotting one croc after another. Some were swimming alongside our boat, others basking in the sun on the banks of the river. Chills went up our spines when we discussed what they're capable of, but we also felt a deep admiration for these incredible creatures that have existed for millions of years. Our afternoon culminated when we saw a group of five crocodiles lying on a muddy embankment right in front of us. We were fascinated by how still they could be, when all of a sudden – faster than lightning – they slipped into the water ... somewhere ... underneath our boat!

After a restful night in the tranquillity of the Mary River Wilderness Retreat, we explored Hardies 4WD Track. In the tropical heat, we passed a cattle station and countless giant termite mounds, and even navigated our way through gushing river crossings. After the previous day's experience, we were certainly not tempted to dip our toes in the water! 99

JEN AND CLINT

PLACES WE GO

WHAT TO DO

- Stay at Mary River Wilderness Retreat, a picturesque eco-resort with campsites and cabins, set on the magical Mary River.
- Explore the interior of the park on the Hardies or Wildman four-wheel-drive tracks.
- Try your luck at landing a barramundi on a fishing cruise of Corroboree Billabong.
- Launch a boat from Rockhole to explore the waterways, or enjoy stunning views over a lily-studded billabong from Couzens Lookout.

» Sunset over the springs

» The town was the setting for We of the Never Never

» *You'd look this happy after spending all day in the thermal springs of Elsey National Parks*

MATARANKA

> Mataranka has an ability to bring people from all walks of life together. It isn't flashy and there is no resort, but you can get a good meal at the pub. And then, of course, there are the hot springs – they're like a spa and their turquoise water is glorious. It's easy to spend hours soaking in them.
>
> **Janet Denton, Marion, South Australia**

Made famous as a harsh and isolated outpost by Jeannie Gunn in her book *We of the Never Never*, Mataranka is now a welcoming Northern Territory outback town south of Katherine, equally famous for its spring-fed thermal pools as its literary history.

Its natural swimming pools in Elsey National Park, such as Bitter Springs and Rainbow Springs, are inviting, warm and crystal clear. Shaded by lush palms, you might even share the water with a friendly turtle. They offer a welcome respite from the heat of the outback, or could be just the place to unwind after a day spent fishing for barramundi on the nearby Roper River.

But you can't escape from the fact that this is 'Never Never' country, a name adopted by the locals in celebration of the place they now hold in Australian folklore. When Aeneas and Jeannie Gunn were posted to Mataranka in 1902 to live on and manage Elsey Station, Jeannie was the first white woman in the area. She published the book as an account of her experience, which lasted only until her husband's death from malarial dysentery in 1903. The book has since sold over a million copies and visitors to Mataranka can experience a replica of the Gunn's original homestead, which was built for the 1982 movie version of the book.

> " The locals of Mataranka, like farmer Jim Sullivan, struck such a chord with us that we often reminisce about them fondly. The town itself is not much more than a tiny main street, its centrepiece being the life-size statues based on Jeannie Gunn's book *We of the Never Never*. The statues not only add character to the town, but they bring the history of the region alive and pay homage to the pioneering settlers who took on such a remote and unforgiving part of the world.
>
> The springs are an absolute must. In the outback heat, they're like a gift from Mother Nature. (And don't worry about crocodiles! They don't inhabit the thermal springs.) Surrounded by the shade of Elsey National Park, the water is like a bath so you don't want to get out! Hanging out with fellow travellers from all over the world, we spent an entire day mesmerised by our lush surroundings, floating around in the crystal-clear waters, and cruising downstream with the current. To our daughter Charli's delight, we even spotted a few turtles!
>
> Our time in Mataranka ended on the Roper River fishing for barramundi. I can't say we had any luck(!) but we were totally captivated by the vibrant outback sunset that lit up the water. "
>
> **JEN AND CLINT**
>
> PLACES WE GO

WHAT TO DO

- Join the twice-daily barramundi feeding at Territory Manor, a unique celebration of the Top End's most famous fish.
- Drop into the Never Never Museum in town, which showcases early settler history alongside that of the region's traditional custodians, the Mangarayi and Yangman people. It also has displays on the Australian Overland Telegraph Line and the North Australia Railway.
- Visit Elsey National Park for a soak in the natural hot springs, or to canoe or fish on the mighty Roper River.

MOUNT BORRADAILE

Occupying a restricted and extremely remote location against the Arnhem Land escarpment, Mount Borradaile is an exclusive piece of land and registered Aboriginal sacred site, harbouring some of the most significant culture and wilderness in the entire country. It's managed by the traditional owners, the Amurdak people, who have inhabited the area for over 50,000 years, but custodian status was also conferred upon 'bushman' Max Davidson in 1986.

Davidson negotiated a lease over 700 square kilometres and, in a joint venture with the local Aboriginal people, invites visitors to experience this timeless land through Davidson's Arnhemland Safaris, a safari lodge and eco-tour. The business provides employment for the local community and injects income into its economy. Access to Mount Borradaile is mostly via light aircraft and can be organised through Davidson's Arnhemland Safaris when booking. Self-drivers are also welcome.

An experience at this living, breathing museum of natural history is like no other; every venture into the wilderness is a lesson you will never forget. With tranquil billabongs, rainforests, floodplains teeming with wildlife, and caves that shelter some of the most significant Aboriginal rock art in the country, it is a region where nature knows no bounds and the country's spectacular heritage is truly and richly unveiled.

> I'll never forget flying over the bushland in Arnhem Land, which felt like it just went on forever. Then all of a sudden a small clearing appeared, and we were descending towards it! We touched down on a tiny airstrip and a man in a safari-style outfit bounded towards us from his old jeep, which looked like it was straight out of a jungle movie. 'Welcome to Mount Borradaile, or Awunbarna, which is the Indigenous name', Max Davidson of Davidson's Arnhemland Safaris said with a huge smile.
>
> Max introduced us to one of the traditional landowners, Charlie, and over the next couple of days they shared what they loved about the area. We were taken on a trek through the sacred site, which is filled with the most beautiful Aboriginal rock art, and includes images of fish, wallabies, emus, handprints and huge Rainbow Serpents. Max pointed out two dynamic figures whose style, he said, went back 20,000 years.
>
> Another highlight was our boat ride on the flood plain, on which Charlie sat up front spotting crocodiles for us (there were many!). As we made our way through the swamplands, the passage opened up to reveal a big rocky watering hole where we sat and enjoyed lunch while fishing for barramundi.
>
> Watching the sun set over the flood plains was truly magical. We sat in silence as the sun slowly dipped beneath the water, all the while absorbing the beauty of this ancient land.

JEN AND CLINT

PLACES WE GO ▸

» *A calm surface – but plenty of crocs underneath!*

WHAT TO DO

- Stay at Davidson's Arnhemland Safaris and allow nature to take care of your itinerary.
- Witness a sunset on a billabong cruise and watch the Mount Borradaile rocks glow in the sinking light.
- Explore Aboriginal rock-art galleries depicting the everyday lives of the local Aboriginal people.
- Discover your inner birdwatcher as thousands of species converge on the wetlands.

It is just such an amazing sight! This great monolith in the middle of nowhere is like a permanent record of the steadfastness and durability of the Aboriginal people who named it. Man-made structures might be great, but there is no better way to really satisfy the soul than to experience a sight like this that has nothing to do with human achievement – it just is.

Christy Prosper, Nundah, Queensland

» *An iconic image, but something you have to see for yourself*

ULURU

Gathering on a viewing platform in the dark, hearing excited whispers around you, you know something special is about to happen. It might still be dark, but you can feel the immense size of the outback around you, and the only thing between the earth and sky is the sacred rock that has started to glow as the breaking sun unveils itself.

First purple, then red, and then with every inch the sun moves up into the sky the rock is further illuminated until the deep orange form of Uluru stands proudly before you in all its glory. Soon the sun is high in the sky and the warmth finally reaches your bones, but you hadn't even realised it was cold. Through the lens of your camera, or your bare eyes, Uluru at sunrise is a true spectacle, and an incredible curtain-raiser for the main event, a walk around its base.

One of the true icons of Australia, Uluru is the spiritual heart of the country and the traditional land of the Anangu people. Their ancient history and culture comes alive on a visit to Uluru–Kata Tjuta National Park, beginning at the cultural centre at the base of Uluru.

A 9-kilometre circuit will take you around the base of the rock, where you can get up close and witness the full scale of this natural wonder, which rises to 348 metres. See Aboriginal rock art that dates back at least 5000 years, and marvel at caves and gullies that have been naturally carved into the walls of the monolith after millions of years.

At the end of the day, as the sun makes its way down the other side of the sky, the rock glows and shifts colour once more. A silence falls over the desert, as people near and far collectively appreciate the sight, and treasure the stories they have been privileged enough to share.

> There's nothing like the first time we saw Uluru. It was a place we had dreamt of visiting all our lives, and we'd seen a million pictures of it in books and on postcards, so to see it up close was quite surreal. No amount of research would prepare us for how imposing it would feel until we stood in front of it. Humbled, we felt like specks of dust.
>
> It has such an incredible energy about it, and the striking red colour of the rock set off by the deep blue sky is spectacular.
>
> We took a walk around the base with a local Aboriginal man who shared stories of how his ancestors lived, and how important the sacred site of Uluru is to his people. He said whenever he was at Uluru, he felt a sense of calm. This was something we felt too and being there we could understand why it's known as the heartbeat of Australia.
>
> We joined friends and family for one of the most memorable nights under the stars you could wish for at the 'Sounds of Silence' dinner. As the sun started to dip below the horizon, Uluru turned into a towering silhouette, with the colours of the sunset throwing pinks and oranges across the desert sky. As night fell, the stars were truly magnificent. This is a sight that's been enjoyed by Aboriginal people for tens of thousands of years, and it was truly a privilege for us to be there.

JEN AND CLINT

PLACES WE GO

WHAT TO DO

- Visit the cultural centre to learn more about Uluru, its traditional owners and its native environment.
- Go on a guided walk with an Anangu Aboriginal guide.
- Take a dot painting workshop to learn the ancient form of western desert Indigenous art.
- Join a Harley-Davidson motorcycle tour around Uluru to experience it from a completely different perspective.
- Enjoy a 'Sounds of Silence' dinner, a five-star dining experience under the stars, with Uluru as the background.

QUEENSLAND

» The local transport in town!

» Under the magnificent starry sky

» Rounding up the cattle in classic style

BIRDSVILLE

You don't get much more off-the-beaten track than Birdsville. In central-west Queensland on the edge of the Simpson Desert, this little outback town with a big heart has a population of only around 120 people, but it's still managed to make a name for itself.

Established to collect tolls from droves of cattle being moved between South Australia and Queensland, Birdsville is dotted with monuments of famous early explorers who passed through on their epic journeys, including Burke and Wills and Captain Charles Sturt.

It now welcomes people who have adventure in their blood and a thirst to explore the real Australian outback. Spend an evening at the iconic Birdsville Hotel and you'll meet a good proportion of the locals, who will happily chat to you and ensure you leave as friends.

The annual Birdsville Races are its biggest tourist drawcard, attracting up to 6000 visitors each September for the two-day horseracing event. Held since 1882, the races are in aid of the Royal Flying Doctor Service.

" The Birdsville Hotel would have to be one of the most famous outback pubs in Australia. We arrived on a Friday and it was filled with locals enjoying a cold beer and a catch-up after their week on the land – they welcomed us like old friends. After meeting the local pilot at the bar, she invited us to go flying over this vast, flat land the following day – it was incredible to take in the size of the enormous cattle stations from the air.

In town for the Bronco Branding festival, we couldn't have had a better taste of what life on the land is all about. Clint even found himself in on the action joining a team of local men in the yards branding the cattle. He was the first to admit he didn't last long, leaving it up to 'some of the toughest men in Australia'.

It wasn't just the locals who made this trip so memorable; it was also our fellow travellers in the campground, like Sully who had been coming here *every year* for the past 50 years. Under the most magnificent starry sky, we joined him at his campfire as he played the harmonica, with the sound of the cattle off in the distance.

Oh, and be sure to check out the Birdsville Bakery – it's quite the treat in such a remote part of the world. You can even order a camel pie! "

JEN AND CLINT

PLACES WE GO

If you like vast expanses of desert all around you, rich red sand dunes as high as houses, waterholes that teem with birdlife after the rains and at other times are hot and dusty from the cattle mustering, rodeos and gymkhanas, and a sky as big as the world, then Birdsville is for you. Its isolation is its charm, and the township has friendly locals for whom it seems nothing is too much trouble.

Eileen Adams, Eltham, Victoria

WHAT TO DO

- Visit for the annual Birdsville Races in September. Most people arrive by air, and the town's red-dirt airstrip fills with small planes. Camping is the only way this tiny town can accommodate the crowds, so pitch a tent and join in the fun.

- Hop in a four-wheel drive and head out to 'Big Red', the largest sand dune in the Simpson Desert (at 40 metres high) and the most impressive of its 1000-plus neighbours.

BOODJAMULLA (LAWN HILL) NATIONAL PARK

An oasis in the outback, Boodjamulla (Lawn Hill) National Park in Queensland's Gulf Country, 3.5 hours north of Mount Isa, might be an adventure to get to, but it's more than worth the effort. Lawn Hill Gorge is the crown in this timeless environment, cut out of ancient red rock, with reflective emerald-green pools, and surrounded by sandstone ranges and dry, semi-arid countryside. It is best discovered on a walking trail that takes you past pandanus palms and giant paperbarks, or by canoe on the tranquil waters themselves.

The lush green vegetation attracts an abundance of birdlife and wildlife, including freshwater crocodiles and turtles on the water's edge. The ancient geology of the landscape reveals some of its secrets with one of the most significant deposits of long-extinct species found in the Riversleigh fossil fields, Australia's most famous fossil site and World Heritage–listed. Considered one of the most important fossil finds in the world, the 100-square-kilometre site is unique for its soft, freshwater limestone that hasn't compressed, meaning that fossils of mammals, reptiles and birds from the Oligocene and Miocene ages, up to 25 million years of age, are still three-dimensional.

For more than 17,000 years the Aboriginal Waanyi people have lived in Boodjamulla, or Rainbow Serpent country. Lawn Hill Gorge is sacred to the Waanyi, who today help manage the park. It was once part of one of Queensland's biggest cattle stations, Lawn Hill Station, until it was returned to the state in 1984.

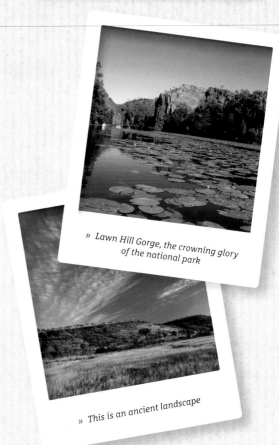

» *Lawn Hill Gorge, the crowning glory of the national park*

» *This is an ancient landscape*

WHAT TO DO

- Take the 3.8 kilometre Indarri Falls walk to the scenic waterfall that separates the upper and middle gorges in Lawn Hill Gorge, and be rewarded with a cool dip at the end.
- Take the bridge across the gorge to discover some of the Waanyi's incredibly rich history within the park at their ancient rock-art gallery Wild Dog Dreaming Art Shelter.
- Camp at the eco-sensitive Adels Grove Camping Park, 10 kilometres downstream from Lawn Hill Gorge and surrounded by a plantation of exotic trees. You can even try to catch a barramundi from Lawn Hill Creek just metres from your campsite.

» Termite mounds stand sentinel along the north road

» *Clint catching a shark (it's not quite Jaws)*

CAPE YORK PENINSULA

Cape York Peninsula is one of Australia's last great frontiers. With 14 million hectares home to over 3000 plant species and 321 bird species, it's a true wilderness that connects adventurers with ancient cultures, unspoiled natural environments and a once-in-a-lifetime experience that includes reaching the northernmost tip of Australia's mainland.

A four-wheel-drive adventure that can be combined with one or many walks, the journey to Cape York Peninsula has almost become a pilgrimage for many Australians, who want the challenge of exploring the vast, remote region of the north and the achievement of making it to the tip.

But it is not all about the final destination. Most travellers beginning in Cairns travel through World Heritage–listed tropical rainforest to reach Laura or Cooktown, from where the four-wheel-drive journey on unsealed roads begins. From Bramwell Junction, the Old Telegraph Track provides an adventure that includes river crossings and World War II history. World-class fishing can be found in the northern rivers of the peninsula, and there are more than enough deserted beaches to ensure your campsites will be crowd-free.

At the end of your long journey, you emerge from rainforest to a carpark, from where the final stretch to the Cape is on foot. A monument marks the occasion of Captain James Cook's arrival in 1770 for his first recorded contact with Aboriginal people. As you claim your own part of this incredible location's history, gaze out towards Possession Island for the same view Captain Cook and the Indigenous people would have had in 1770.

" We spent a few weeks exploring Cape York Peninsula right up to the most northern tip of Australia, where we'll never forget watching one of the most vibrant sunsets we'd ever seen.

Driving through some of the remote townships was a real eye-opener, especially when you see how high the water levels reach during the wet season. We spent many a day chatting to locals about how they live with limited supplies when the roads are often cut off for weeks. Many told us that while the rains may cause havoc at times, they're also magical to witness and part of what they love about the region.

Along the way we stopped off at a historic cattle station that was the home of pioneering settlers. Standing there with our four-month-old daughter in the scorching heat drove home just how tough they would have had to be, living out here with none of today's creature comforts, and no contact with the rest of the world.

Even though we had plenty of air-conditioned hotels to stay in along the way, there was something about the remoteness of the place that made us feel intrepid. We saw snakes crossing the red dusty roads and crocodiles on the banks of rivers, and even ate a witchetty grub while we were on a trek with local Indigenous guide Willie Gordon! (They taste like almonds when cooked, if you're wondering.) This is definitely a place for anyone who loves an adventure. "

JEN AND CLINT

PLACES WE GO

WHAT TO DO

- Stock up on fuel and supplies and meet the locals in Cooktown.
- Visit the Aboriginal rock-art galleries of the Cape, which have been rated by Unesco among the top ten most significant art sites in the world.
- Find your inner birdwatcher: with such a range of habitats on the peninsula, it's an exciting birding destination for anyone.

CARNARVON NATIONAL PARK

Hidden in the central highlands of Queensland's outback, Carnarvon National Park is tucked in like a treasure, with spectacular Carnarvon Gorge as its masterpiece. An area of rich and lush vegetation, some of the finest Aboriginal rock art in the country and the 160-million-year-old Carnarvon Gorge, this national park is a remote and breathtaking natural wilderness.

Where the earth has been carved open by Carnarvon Creek to create the immense gorge, 200-metre-high white sandstone cliffs tower over a natural oasis of rich vegetation where hundreds of plants thrive, including some ancient species. The permanent water source attracts wildlife and over 175 species of birds. You might be lucky and spot a platypus playing in the shallows, and eastern grey kangaroos are a regular encounter. Side gorges have also been formed, complete with waterfalls, moss gardens and rainforest.

The park itself is around 160 kilometres wide from east to west, and contrasts with the lush oasis of the gorge with pockets of grassy plateaus, sandstone cliffs and bluffs. It was named in the 1840s after a place in Wales by the first European to traverse the region, Thomas Mitchell.

It's also a significant Dreamtime area. The park's traditional owners are the Bidjara, Karingbal and Kara Kara people, whose lives and culture are represented in three rock-art galleries at Carnarvon Gorge. In the Art Gallery, dating back around 4000 years, 62 metres of wall depict more than 2000 ochre stencils, freehand paintings and engravings. The larger Cathedral Cave has even more extensive works, including representations of human hands, spears and boomerangs.

» Jaw-dropping view over the park

WHAT TO DO

- Visit the park's three rock-art galleries, all reached via walking trails. Baloon Cave is the easiest to get to (30 minutes), Cathedral Cave is the most difficult (five to six hours return).
- Hike the network of bushwalking trails to discover Carnarvon Gorge. Most start near the visitor centre and range from easy, one-hour return walks to three- to four-hour hikes visiting some of the more unique attractions of the park.

Not only the oldest living rainforest on earth, but the most enchanting ecosystem I have ever visited. From snorkelling in the crystal-clear Mossman Gorge (alongside numerous terrapins) to 'jungle surfing' through the treetop canopy, the Daintree is a true paradise. My husband and I stayed at Silky Oaks Lodge in amazing, luxury tree-house accommodation. Other highlights included tasting Daintree Estates chocolate and tropical fruit wines.

Christina Salt, South Guildford, Western Australia

» *At the edge of the rainforest you'll find unspoilt beaches*

» *You'll feel small surrounded by the oldest living rainforest on earth*

DAINTREE RAINFOREST & CAPE TRIBULATION

An enduring reminder of the power of nature, the Daintree Rainforest is a living treasure, surviving and indeed flourishing in the country's far north as if time had stood still around it.

The oldest living rainforest on earth at around 140 million years old, the World Heritage–listed site is about 12,000 square kilometres of dense jungle with magnificent primitive species and rich biodiversity. Tropical rainforest meets eucalypt forest, wetlands and mangroves, and this incredible region is the only place in the world where two World Heritage sites meet: the Daintree grows all the way to the Great Barrier Reef (*see* p. 173) on the coast.

The Daintree's traditional owners are the Eastern Kuku Yalanji Aboriginal people, for whom the landscape holds significant spiritual value. Part of the ancient rainforest is protected within Daintree National Park, and is drained by the Daintree River, a cruise along which reveals the jungle habitats of a vast array of birds, reptiles (including large crocodiles) and other wildlife.

Cross the river on the cable ferry and enter the wonderland of Cape Tribulation, a headland within the rainforest made famous as the site where Captain James Cook's *Endeavour* hit the reef in 1770, causing severe damage. Today it is a place where visitors can experience staying overnight in the jungle and enjoy unspoiled beaches framed by the rainforest. But it is still very much an off-the-beaten-track destination where nature is king.

"As soon as we jumped on board the cable ferry, we were ushered across the crocodile-infested Daintree River, and welcomed into the Daintree Rainforest. As we navigated our way through the undulating terrain, all we wanted to do was look up at the trees towering over us.

Twenty-five kilometres up the road we were driving on the famous, four-wheel-drive-only Bloomfield Track. Our trip was quite the bumpy off-road adventure, and we prayed there were no other cars coming towards us! But with some sturdy concentration by our guide Bart at the wheel, we made our way to Bloomfield Falls. Here we went on a walking tour with traditional landowners and sisters, Gloria and Agnes Walker, who are members of the Kuku Yalanji clan, which has lived in the area for tens of thousands of years.

As they showed us around, teaching us all about bush tucker, they said how sharing their culture with the world was a dream come true. After growing up in the region, they want to keep the stories of their ancestors alive.

Just as it was time to leave and we thought we'd gotten away without sampling any 'live' bush tucker, another sister, Kathleen, produced a handful of green ants. She told us about their medicinal uses: you can rub them on your body for good health … or you can eat them!

So did we? Why, of course! They actually weren't too bad: a little zesty and a lot like lemons!"

JEN AND CLINT

PLACES WE GO

DID YOU KNOW?

- The Daintree is named after Richard Daintree, an Australian geographer and photographer (1832–1878).
- The rainforest contains 30 per cent of the frog, reptile and marsupial species in Australia and 65 per cent of the bat and butterfly species. Eighteen per cent of bird species and more than 12,000 species of insect can all be found in the area, which comprises 0.1 per cent of Australia's land mass.
- Mossman Gorge is a popular attraction in the southern section of the park, around 80 kilometres north of Cairns. It is a natural swimming pool with lush rainforest and creek scenery, massive boulders, walking trails and picnic areas.
- The four-wheel-drive Bloomfield Track goes from Cape Tribulation to Cooktown, crossing creeks and venturing through pristine jungle terrain with the roaring Bloomfield Falls as the ultimate reward.

FRASER ISLAND

Fraser Island is a place of timeless beauty and the ultimate off-road adventure where the beach is the highway and sandy tracks lead to a circular route of spectacular inland lakes. Don't miss swimming in Lake McKenzie, floating down crystal-clear Eli Creek and traipsing through magnificent rainforests. Fraser has shipwrecks and wildlife, resorts and great camping, and combines relaxation with adventure. It's an absolute Australian gem.

Miriam Blaker, Hurstbridge, Victoria

The world's largest sand island beckons those who are up for a bit of adventure. With miles and miles of sandy beaches to explore by four-wheel drive or on foot, Fraser Island is a haven for nature-lovers, campers and wildlife enthusiasts.

Stretching over 123 kilometres in length, just off the southern Queensland coast, Fraser Island is World Heritage listed for its natural and cultural value and exceptional beauty. It is the only place in the world where rainforests grow directly out of the sand at elevations of 200 metres, framing crystal-clear creeks and more than 100 inland freshwater lakes.

The island's Indigenous owners, the Butchulla people, call it K'gari (paradise) – and it is easy to see why. Your trip to paradise could include sailing next to turtles, dugongs and dolphins, tackling the day-long Lake McKenzie circuit walk, spotting humpback whales between August and October, and exploring the S.S. *Maheno* shipwreck. Seventy Five Mile Beach is home to hundreds of four-wheel-drive sand tracks. It's like a sandy highway used to get between the beach and the rainforest, the lakes and the ancient, coloured sand cliffs of the Pinnacles.

At the end of the day, when the sun sets over the immense sand dunes, sparkling lakes and pristine rainforest, wind down at a luxury eco-resort or in your own tent under the stars.

" It's pretty incredible to be able to drive on the sandy beaches of the biggest sand island in the world. At times there was no-one else on the beach as we navigated our way along the sand, even around rocks with the ocean splashing up around our tyres!

To catch a bird's-eye view of this stunning place, we took a scenic flight – and the pilot turned up with board shorts on! We commented that he would have to be one of the luckiest pilots in the world to have such an office. From the air, you can see how the rainforest grows out of the vast sand dunes, how the island is peppered with countless inland lakes, and how all roads lead to the ocean.

Surrounded by lush rainforest and never-ending sand dunes, we felt so lucky to be camping under the shade of the trees, and treated to the truly stunning scene that unfolded before us as the sun went down over Lake McKenzie. Soon after, the moon lit up the lake, with not a ripple on the water. "

JEN AND CLINT

PLACES WE GO

WHAT TO DO

- Go for a dip in Champagne Pools, large saltwater rockpools that are like natural jacuzzis.
- Take a scenic flight for a full-scale view of the World Heritage–listed sand island.
- Hire a four-wheel drive or bring your own to tackle the natural sandy highway of Seventy Five Mile Beach.

» Tracks on the main beach

The day I snorkelled the Great Barrier Reef was the best day of my life. Everyone needs to experience what it's like to be surrounded by such natural, surreal beauty. The colours, the sunlight on the water, the warmth of the Queensland sun on your back and the dreamlike creatures to be seen make this place a top bucket-list destination. It makes you really appreciate our earth.

Elizabeth Berezy, Melbourne, Victoria

» *The reef*

» *Exhilarated after a dive at Balt Reef*

» *This aerial view shows that the Great Barrier Reef is truly deserving its title as one of the wonders of the world*

GREAT BARRIER REEF

One of Australia's, and the world's, biggest living treasures, the Great Barrier Reef has accumulated all kinds of labels, awards and titles to recognise its significance, but no amount of words can do it justice. The world's largest coral reef system, this natural masterpiece is so big, it can be seen from outer space.

Stretching 2000 kilometres down the Queensland coastline from the tip of Cape York (*see* p. 165) to Bundaberg, it is made up of around 3000 individual reefs and coral cays, and crowned with hundreds of breathtaking tropical islands boasting some of the world's best beaches.

Of course, its wonder lies under the water and snorkellers and scubadivers are rewarded with visions that almost defy belief. The world's largest collection of colourful coral gardens dazzle the eyes, over 1500 species of tropical fish swim amongst turtles, dolphins, rays, sharks and molluscs, and the mighty humpback whale is an annual visitor, using the reef as its spectacular breeding ground.

The reef itself dates back around 20 million years. Aboriginal people occupied the areas around the reef for around 40,000 years, fishing and hunting its waters between the islands. The first documented sightings of the reef were by French explorers, but it was Captain James Cook who sailed the *Endeavour* the length of the reef in 1770, striking part of it near Cape Tribulation in the north and needing six weeks to make repairs to the ship in order to continue.

Today the reef is one of the world's biggest tourist attractions, and can be accessed by a number of gateway coastal towns or from inhabited islands. Snorkelling, diving and flying over the reef are some of the most popular ways to discover it.

> As lovers of scuba diving, the Great Barrier Reef is one of our favourite places in Australia. We've enjoyed so many truly magnificent experiences both snorkelling and diving in all different areas of the reef, but one of the stand-outs was when we visited it from Airlie Beach in Far North Queensland. We headed by boat two hours offshore to a place called Bait Reef on the Outer Reef.
>
> First we took a leisurely dive exploring a couple of bommies. The waters were like a warm fish tank, filled with hundreds of tiny, brightly coloured fish, and beautiful coral gardens. We even saw a couple of reef sharks, which is always a highlight, as they carry a particular energy, different from other fish.
>
> After coming out of the water, our divemaster asked if we wanted to experience the reef in a whole different light – both literally and figuratively! – with a night dive, which is when the larger fish come out! An opportunity too good to resist, we took it on. Before we knew it, we were back-flipping off the boat in complete darkness, and descending into a whole new world. With only the light from our torches, our senses came alive, and we felt every ripple around us as the fish darted to and fro. As we navigated our way around the bommies, we can't say our hearts weren't in our mouths!
>
> Night or day, the Great Barrier Reef is a treasure for the world, and a place that we personally hold dear to our hearts.

JEN AND CLINT

PLACES WE GO

DID YOU KNOW?

- The Great Barrier Reef was named one of the Seven Natural Wonders of the World.
- In area, it is greater in size than the United Kingdom, Switzerland and the Netherlands combined.
- It was awarded World Heritage status in 1981.
- A large part of the reef is within the Great Barrier Reef Marine Park, protecting it from the impacts of fishing and tourism.

MAGNETIC ISLAND

Just 8 kilometres off the coast of Townsville, but a world away in spectacular natural beauty, Magnetic Island is a jewel in the crown of the Great Barrier Reef Marine Park. Two-thirds of the island is covered in national park, and, surrounded as it is by the Great Barrier Reef, the entire island offers a protected, stunning environment both on and off shore.

With 23 bays and beaches, you are spoilt for choice as to how to spend your time enjoying them. With beach horseriding, snorkel trails along fringing reef, watersports and fishing, every day offers the possibility of a new adventure.

You can discover 'Maggie' on foot by tackling some of the 25 kilometres of walking trails on the island, which wind through pristine bushland to lush rainforest. The largest population of koalas in northern Australia live in the wild here, so you might spot one while admiring the view from one of the many lookout points.

The island was once part of the mainland until sea levels rose around 7500 years ago. Its traditional owners, the Yunbenun people, lived in seasonal camps in many of the bays, and travelled between the island and mainland in canoes. The first European to the island was Captain James Cook, who said that the island interfered with his compass with a kind of magnetic force, hence its present name (modern testing has disproved his theory).

The island was an important defensive post during World War II and today, many remnants from the war can still be found along national park walking trails.

> Arriving on Magnetic Island is like being welcomed into a whole new world. It feels like it's found that balance where humans and wildlife live together in idyllic harmony. We've not only been to 'Maggie' to film our TV series, but for a family holiday with friends and their children. We have so many happy memories, like watching the magnificent sunsets over Horseshoe Bay, kayaking, and trekking with the kids on the Forts Walk trail, spotting koalas along the way.
>
> One of our most treasured memories was on a boat ride exploring the marine park with local skipper Adam, whose love for his backyard was infectious. He grew up on the island after his family made the move when he was a young boy. Today he is proud to say he is giving his four children the same idyllic life. The kind, he said, where kids can run free because the island is their backyard, where you don't have to worry about locking your door, and where on any given day you can see whales, turtles, dugongs and other wildlife. Indeed, while we were talking, we were holding fish in the air feeding white-bellied sea eagles that were swooping down and eating out of our hands!
>
> Our family holiday ended with breakfast at Bungalow Bay Koala Village with a bunch of travellers from all over the world and a very spirited wildlife keeper named Tony. He delighted in sharing his love of wildlife with a lively presentation of all manner of slippery creatures and cuddly koalas!

JEN AND CLINT

PLACES WE GO

WHAT TO DO

- Don't miss the 2 kilometre Forts Walk trail, an excellent opportunity to catch superb views over the island, spot a koala and discover some of Magnetic Island's World War II history.
- Head to Horseshoe Bay for all the watersports you can imagine, including sailing, kayaking and paddleboating.
- Grab fins and a mask and head out on one of two snorkel trails – one in Nelly Bay and one in Geoffrey Bay – to discover Great Barrier Reef treasures under the water.

This well-kept secret offers something for everyone: scenic bush walks; native animals you can feed; amazing restaurants, cafes and local taverns; warm blue waters just off the Great Barrier Reef. If it's relaxation, nightlife, nature, watersports or fishing you're after, then this place is for you. The island caters for families, young and old, backpackers and other tourists. A definite must-see island paradise.

Kara Voznaks, Newmarket, Queensland

» *A local*

Although its popularity is increasing, Mission Beach is still a hidden gem that makes you feel immediately relaxed. I always feel like I have gone back in time, away from the rush and insanity of day-to-day life. The sun shines. The beaches are white. Life is good at Mission Beach.

Helen Gillman, Broadbeach, Queensland

» *Camp on the beach*

» *Your mission, should you choose to accept it, is to enjoy the World Heritage–listed surrounds*

MISSION BEACH

Located between the reef and the rainforest, Queensland's small coastal town of Mission Beach is relaxed and even a little bit sleepy, but dig beneath the surface and there is plenty of adventure to be found.

In a place of spectacular beauty, Mission Beach couldn't ask for a better position. Its front yard is the mighty Great Barrier Reef, so there's reef diving and snorkelling offshore, and tropical islands can be reached in a matter of minutes. A glorious beach with 14 kilometres of golden sand dotted with palm trees also welcomes you. And its backyard? World Heritage–listed wet tropical rainforest, with walking trails, waterfalls and lush habitats for species like the cassowary.

Named for the Aboriginal mission set up in the area in 1914, the town has rebuilt itself after several devastating cyclones, most recently cyclone Yasi. Each time it's emerged as a thriving tourist destination thanks to its natural assets and friendly, laid-back locals.

Its proximity to such incredible natural features ensures it is a hotspot on the map for adventure lovers, who come to the area for spectacular skydiving, whitewater rafting, diving, snorkelling, fishing, mountain-biking and bushwalking. The region's rich Indigenous history can be discovered in the hinterland, where generations of the Janbanbarra Jirrbal Rainforest people have lived, and still conserve their culture and land in this magnificent setting.

> " Mission Beach is blessedly sandwiched between World Heritage rainforest and the World Heritage–listed Great Barrier Reef, and thankfully has defied major development. It's an old-fashioned coastal town in the tropics, with just a few local restaurants, palm trees swaying in the breeze and silky sand between your toes.
>
> From the beach, you can see Dunk Island sitting proudly amongst about a dozen islands, all part of the Family Islands group. If you keep your eyes peeled you might also see turtles, dugongs, dolphins and whales swimming about offshore. We took a boat ride across to one of the islands for a picnic, and on other days, back on the mainland, trekked through the rainforest, navigated our way across a gushing creek and swam under a waterfall with local Indigenous guide Caroline. She shared the story of her family growing up there and their escape from the Aboriginal mission, after which Mission Beach was named.
>
> We had the most perfect day to scuba dive on the Great Barrier Reef, which is just a 20-minute boat ride away. The water is literally crystal-clear and sparkling; you can see the colourful coral and marine life from the surface! Underwater, we saw hundreds of different coloured fish, a leopard sea cucumber and even a couple of reef sharks!
>
> There's something special about Mission Beach. It's taken a battering over the years due to cyclones, and yet it and its passionate locals remain resilient. "

JEN AND CLINT

PLACES WE GO

WHAT TO DO

- Visit the Family Islands, which include Dunk Island, by water taxi. They lie just off the coast of Mission Beach.
- Don't miss a snorkelling or diving trip to the Great Barrier Reef, literally on your doorstep.
- Drop into the local Sunday market, held on the beachfront and offering everything from arts and crafts, jewellery, plants, fresh local fruit and vegetables, and other local produce.

PORT DOUGLAS

Port Douglas is like the popular kid in school: blessed with amazing looks, surrounded by natural wonders, and stylish from head to toe. Even the locals here feel like they are on a permanent tropical holiday.

One of Australia's most northern holiday resorts, Port Douglas boomed as a tourist town after businessman Christopher Skase developed the Sheraton Mirage in the mid-1980s. The rest of the country, and indeed the world, also recognised the town's beauty and things took off. With the Great Barrier Reef (*see* p. 173) on its doorstep, and the Daintree (*see* p. 169) in its backyard, Port Douglas couldn't do much wrong and soon it was a thriving resort town buzzing with cafes, bars and, these days, boutiques, galleries and fine-dining establishments. Pockets of land located along stunning Four Mile Beach fetched millions of dollars as new resorts started to move in, and the sleepy little village became the sophisticated socialite we know today.

Tucked away at the end of a peninsula around an hour's drive north of Cairns, Port Douglas has a natural harbour and marina on one side of the village, and the beach on the other. In between, the township at the bottom of Flagstaff Hill centres on Macrossan Street, with holiday accommodation and chic villas nestled on either side. The town comes alive with visitors frequenting the many dining establishments, parks, bars, cafes and boutiques lining the street and waterfront. Those same visitors enjoy the reef and rainforest on the plethora of tours available from town.

" Palm trees swaying in the breeze, that stunning Four Mile Beach, the magic of the Great Barrier Reef: we think Port Douglas is a stunner. It's always high on our list when we're looking for an escape to the tropics. Spoilt with both the lush Daintree and the Great Barrier Reef, the whole region is Mother Nature at her finest, and makes for a holiday wonderland.

We've enjoyed some beautiful trips out on the reef, both diving and snorkelling. Swimming amongst hundreds of tropical fish and stunning coral, the waters are so warm you barely need a wetsuit.

There are so many fantastic restaurants in town, but one of our favourites without a doubt is Nautilus. As you walk up the stairs, it feels like you're heading into a rainforest to dine under the stars. While the seafood is superb, it's the ambience of this place that blows us away, which sums up beautiful Port Douglas perfectly. *"*

JEN AND CLINT

PLACES WE GO

WHAT TO DO

- Walk the length of Four Mile Beach. Nothing will invigorate you more than passing lines of palm trees on one side and the Coral Sea on the other as you stretch your legs along this iconic strip of beach.
- Visit the Wildlife Habitat Port Douglas, a leading environmental experience allowing you to get up close and personal with a range of native flora and fauna, and even have 'breakfast with the birds'.
- Attend the Sunday markets that are held in Anzac Park weekly, selling arts, crafts, food and drink, all with a distinctly local flavour.
- Watch the sun set over the water and the dive boats return from the reef from On the Inlet restaurant with a bucket of prawns and a cold drink. You even get to watch a 250-kilogram groper fish named George be fed daily at 5pm!

Port Douglas combines luxury with adventure and nature. You can stay in a five-star resort or rent a stunning holiday home. The restaurants are amazing, and there is always so much to do – explore the Daintree, dive the Great Barrier Reef, take a boat trip, play a round of golf, or just relax on the beach!

Kasey Brunt, Parap, Northern Territory

» *The scenery is just as good in the ocean*

» *Not much has changed since Captain James Cook landed here in 1770*

SEVENTEEN SEVENTY

Seventeen Seventy is Queensland's little secret. Beating the crowds and box jellyfish of Cairns, the coral reefs, beaches and fishing here are breathtaking. Camping by the beach, you might even spot a whale or dolphin as they meander by. Captain Cook's adventures put this place on the map and made its history and name.

**Nicola Thomson,
Sunshine Coast, Queensland**

The town of Seventeen Seventy might have been the birthplace of Queensland and the second place on Australian soil that Captain James Cook set foot, but not too much has happened since then, making this idyllic beach village one of Queensland's best-kept secrets.

Named for the year that Captain Cook stepped ashore, Seventeen Seventy is nestled in an area rich in wildlife, with picturesque views in every direction. There are not many beaches in the 'sunshine state' that you can have all to yourself, but there's a good chance you'll find solitude here. The town sits on a peninsula surrounded by the Coral Sea and Bustard Bay on three sides, and it's said to be one of the only places on the Australian coast where you can watch the sun rise and set over the ocean.

Its neighbouring seaside village Agnes Water boasts the most northerly surf beach in Queensland, and hosts the annual Seventeen Seventy longboard surfing competition. Seventeen Seventy's small marina is the gateway to the southern Great Barrier Reef and Lady Musgrave Island, but the real attraction of this town lies in its under-development, leaving it to be a quaint and beautiful beach paradise for the few who have discovered it.

» *It's all about the outdoors*

» *You might even get a beach to yourself*

WHAT TO DO

- Join in the fun at the annual Seventeen Seventy Festival, during which a re-enactment of Captain Cook's *Endeavour* landing takes place.
- Go fishing, kayaking, swimming, surfing, snorkelling … This region is all about the great outdoors, and with an estimated 300 days of sunshine each year, you can try everything under the sun.
- Explore the extensive four-wheel-drive tracks in the region that lead through subtropical rainforests and the hinterland, which you'll probably have all to yourself.

SUNSHINE COAST

A perennial favourite amongst holidaymakers, the Sunshine Coast offers an escape just north of Brisbane with superb beaches, a laid-back lifestyle, subtropical rainforests, rivers, lakes, and charming towns and villages. This is the sort of place that can be as adventurous or relaxed as you want it to be. Blessed with warm sunshine for most of the year, it is guaranteed to soothe your body and soul.

With the clear Coral Sea lapping at its shores, and the cool, crisp bush of the hinterland inland from its beaches, the Sunshine Coast is perfect for the whole family, thanks to its range of attractions and activities, and its natural wonders.

Several sub-regions are ready to be explored, from stylish Noosa with its trendy shops, everglades and endless dining options, to the central beaches of Mooloolaba. Back from the beaches, the peace and solitude of the hinterland and dramatic Glass House Mountains offer a retreat rich in Indigenous history and breathtaking landscapes.

Surfing, sailing, kayaking, abseiling and fishing are just some of the everyday options on the Sunshine Coast, and have been since the end of World War II when the timber and cattle industries of the region gave way to tourism. And with more national parks than any other region in Queensland, the natural wonders in the area will be protected for generations to come.

"Queensland's Sunshine Coast is one of our treasured holiday spots. For us it's home to the good life, which means plenty of sun, sand and a healthy outdoorsy lifestyle. It's the perfect place to enjoy simple family holidays, and we always return home recharged.

We've stayed in many places right up the coast and loved them all. One of our favourite spots is Noosa, where there's nothing better than that first morning of our holiday when we throw on our runners and go for a jog through the national park under a lush canopy of trees, hugging the side of the ocean that stretches out as far as the eye can see.

There are just so many stunning beaches to choose from in this region. We've enjoyed many afternoons splashing around in the sheltered waters of Noosa's Main Beach, and, when we've felt like something a little wilder, bodysurfing on Sunshine Beach, not far away. After our first swim of a holiday, you'll usually find us devouring a coffee (or a cold beer!) in one of our favourite cafes right on the beach in Noosa, or enjoying a more relaxed dinner in the charming strip shops at Sunshine Beach.

We've had so many adventures on the Sunshine Coast – from sailing to scuba diving, even abseiling in the state forest – but no matter what we do, we always find time to sit and just take it all in. It's a real tonic."

JEN AND CLINT

PLACES WE GO

WHAT TO DO

- Hit the stylish streets of Noosa and join the cafe culture along sophisticated Hastings Street, parallel to Main Beach. The annual Noosa International Food and Wine Festival is not to be missed if you are in town at the right time.
- Spend a couple of days exploring the art galleries in the hinterland and browse the Eumundi markets.
- Take the whole family to kid-friendly attractions such as Australia Zoo in Beerwah, and Underwater World in Mooloolaba.

It's natural, unspoilt and very special ... the glorious Sunshine Coast of Queensland! From climbing Mount Coolum, to discovering the national park at Noosa, to cooling down in the hinterland – there are endless places to enjoy. Don't forget to visit Australia Zoo, browse the Eumundi markets and look at the art galleries in Noosa. The beaches in this part of the world are spectacular and the water is always warm!

Petra Burton, Jerrabomberra, New South Wales

» *Unspoilt coastline*

» ***Your biggest challenge on the Sunshine Coast will be deciding on a beach***

» Australia's most northern pub

» One of the traditional owners of the island

THURSDAY & HORN ISLANDS

Journey beyond Cape York to Thursday Island, the heart of the Torres Strait Islands. Steeped in history and living culture, it is an island where tradition and heritage play a pivotal role in everyday life, and ocean views, native flora and fauna and spectacular wildlife will charm you as you immerse yourself in island life.

Thirty-nine kilometres off the coast of Cape York (*see* p. 165) and around 4 kilometres in diameter, Thursday Island is the administrative and commercial centre for the Torres Strait Islands, and has been populated for thousands of years by Melanesian Torres Strait Islanders. Its traditional owners, the Kaurareg people, call the island 'Waibe'.

Thursday boasts four hotels, various accommodation styles, cafes and restaurants and its major drawcard is its laid-back tropical atmosphere and rich heritage.

The Queensland government set up an outpost on the island in 1877 and soon it became a lucrative pearling destination, attracting people from many cultures to make their fortune. The pearling industry has declined today, but the multicultural population remains.

As Australia's northernmost township, Thursday Island became an important military base during World War II. In 1942 civilians were evacuated from the island and residents of Japanese origin were interned. Luckily the island was not bombed, but nearby Horn Island suffered enormous devastation. A visit to Horn Island is well worth it to explore its extensive World War II history as an operational air base. It has a fascinating museum and historical sites for World War II enthusiasts. It's only 15 minutes away from Thursday Island by ferry.

" Exploring both Thursday Island and its close neighbour Horn Island was one of the most interesting trips we've ever done in Australia. The region is filled with so much history that many Australians don't know about. It really is worth a visit.

We loved our afternoon on Thursday Island sitting in Australia's most northern pub chatting to the locals. As soon as we took a seat at the bar, they came up and welcomed us to their home. There's a famous saying around these parts about the pace at which things happen on Thursday Island: when it happens, it happens!

While Thursday Island was spared bombing during World War II, its neighbour Horn Island took a real pounding, and played a major role in the defence of Australia. It was a privilege to spend the day with local woman Vanessa who runs the museum on Horn. She took us on a tour of the island, which is filled with World War II relics, including an old gun pit, slit trenches and a command centre, from which soldiers defended against Japanese air raids in the sweltering heat.

We were lucky enough to meet one of the surviving members of the Torres Strait Island battalion, Joshua. He spoke of his time defending Australia with a strong love for his country. As we were leaving, he asked if he could bless our daughter (who was four months old at the time) for a long and healthy life. It is this spirit that we felt so warmly during our time here. "

JEN AND CLINT

PLACES WE GO

DID YOU KNOW?

- After World War II ended, Thursday Island reinstated a no-footwear policy in respect for the ancient spirits believed to inhabit the island.
- The islanders predominantly speak Torres Strait creole, followed by the Mabuiag language and English. The Indigenous language is Kaiwalgau Ya.
- As the closest operational air base to New Guinea, Horn Island was home to around 5000 servicemen and – women, and was bombed eight times by the Japanese during World War II.

Australia's own island paradise. Crystal-clear blue-green water, endless skies and lovely warm weather. Heaven.

Caitlin Burman, Geelong, Victoria

THE WHITSUNDAYS

Lying in the heart of one of our greatest national treasures, the Great Barrier Reef (*see* p. 173), the Whitsunday islands are its crowning glory. These 74 tropical islands prove that the region's beauty is just as rich above water as below it. It's one of the most prized and revered natural destinations in Australia.

With so many islands to discover and explore, many of them completely secluded, the choice of where to stay and what to do is almost endless. But you can't leave this incredible environment without taking a peek under the water at the pristine reef, finding an isolated bay and settling in for a beach picnic, or trekking the national park trails that cover many of the islands.

From the resorts on Hamilton Island to the white silica sands of Whitehaven Bay, the heart-shaped reef and incredible marine life, the Whitsundays are best explored by foot, by plane and, of course, by boat.

Named after Captain James Cook recorded his sighting of the islands in his diary as 'Whitsunday Passage', the passage wasn't actually discovered until Whit Monday, as the International Date Line had not yet been established. Sailing through the islands is still one of the most popular ways to discover them, and many visitors today would have the same view of the beautiful passage that Cook enjoyed in 1770.

WHAT TO DO

- Snorkel or dive from any number of sites around the Whitsundays for some of the world's best underwater experiences.
- Spend some time on Hamilton Island, the commercial heart of the islands and where resorts, shops, restaurants, bars, cafes and the airport can all be found.
- Get pampered at one of the many day spas on the islands; relaxation is the name of the game here.
- Learn about the Whitsundays' original inhabitants, the Ngaro people, and follow the Whitsunday Ngaro Sea Trail walk to discover their history and culture.

» *Sailing with Jesse Martin*

Hamilton Island is without doubt the ultimate getaway! Perched on the edge of the Great Barrier Reef and nestled among the Whitsunday Islands, it offers the discerning traveller an experience of a lifetime. With stunning coral reefs, inviting beaches and perfect weather, this destination has to be at the top of everyone's bucket list ... just add champagne and ice!

Viv Chelin, Cooma, New South Wales

» Dinosaurs left their mark on Winton

» Amo's Wall

» Lark Quarry, one of Queensland's hidden gems

WINTON

For a small outback town, Winton packs a punch when it comes to history and Australian culture. Located in Queensland's interior, 1153 kilometres from Brisbane, and with a population of less than 1000, this quaint town, largely settled by sheep and cattle farmers, has been put on the map thanks to bush poetry, aviation and dinosaurs.

A.B. 'Banjo' Paterson wrote his most famous poem 'Waltzing Matilda' at nearby Dagworth Station, and the very first performance of the ballad was at the North Gregory Hotel in Winton. Said to be based on Combo Waterhole, 132 kilometres out of town, the song has inspired the region to be named 'Matilda Country'. In addition to that, the Waltzing Matilda Centre was opened in 1998, the only centre in the world dedicated to a song. The region celebrates the bush poem that shaped so much of Australian culture on Waltzing Matilda Day, held annually in town.

Winton also played a significant role in the formation of Australia's national airline, Qantas, in 1920. The first office for the airline was registered here and the inaugural board meeting was held at the Winton Club in 1921. The town is proud of the part it played in the airline's birth, which is documented at the Qantilda Museum within the Waltzing Matilda Centre.

In 1962, Winton found itself on the world stage when fossilised footprints of a dinosaur stampede were discovered at nearby Lark Quarry. The discovery was monumental, and further excavation work revealed 3300 dinosaur tracks belonging to two herds. The largest known stampede on earth, it had been perfectly preserved for over 95 million years in the stone. Today it is carefully protected and accessible to everyone, to see and learn the dramatic story behind the event.

" For us it's always the people we meet along the way that bring a trip alive, and our time in Winton was packed with colourful characters. Take Gloria, for instance, a local bush poet who's busy keeping Banjo Paterson's legacy alive. She visited us at our campsite, and over billy tea and my mum's homemade scones, we spent the afternoon listening to her spontaneous poems about the region, including this one about our travels around Australia:

> The next stop might be different, it could be pouring rain
> But keep your head above water boys, because then you'll go on again
> Don't forget to smell the gidgee and marvel at the gums
> When you're near a creek, get out and have some fun
> It's fine to climb a hill sometimes, there aren't many hills around here
> But when you reach the top, you feel like dinosaurs could still be near

But it's not actually Banjo Paterson that encouraged us to put Winton in this book; it's Lark Quarry. We'd never even heard of the place before we visited Winton, even though it's home to the world's only ever recorded dinosaur stampede. We met local guide Paul, who also runs the local pub; he has been on many digs, and excitedly ushered us to the site. When we asked him if he'd like to time travel to see the dinosaurs, he answered: 'I'd give a king's ransom to step back in time and see a dinosaur for a day.' "

JEN AND CLINT

PLACES WE GO

WHAT TO DO

- Visit Waltzing Matilda Centre, dedicated to one of Australia's most famous songs.
- See evidence of the biggest known dinosaur stampede in the world at Lark Quarry Dinosaur Trackways.
- Be amazed by Arno's Wall, an eccentric and marvellous construction made by local man Arno Grotjahn from concrete, rock and almost every household item you could think of, including sewing machines and motorbikes.

TASMANIA

» *The postcard-perfect location*

» *The bay's famous white sand, red-lichen-covered rocks and turquoise water*

BAY OF FIRES

» *Sunset lights up the yachts*

In a country full of pristine coastline, the Bay of Fires in north-east Tasmania stands out for its unique combination of white sand, turquoise water and red-lichen-splashed boulders that many think the stretch of sand was named after. It was actually named by Captain Tobias Furneaux in 1773 when he saw the many fires Aboriginal people were burning on its shore.

Today it is an area that sums up Tasmania's beauty perfectly – untouched, unique and postcard-perfect. It is protected within a conservation area, so development has remained at a minimum. Positioned just north of the quaint fishing village of St Helens, it stretches for 13 kilometres, and is popular with campers, beachgoers, birdwatchers and people who simply come to stare at the views.

Take a walk along the squeaky white beach, brave the cold waters of the Tasman Sea with a surfboard, or join one of the well-regarded guided walks that have been established here to show off the scenery.

A drive or walk along the coast might treat you to a glimpse of whales or dolphins, while the rockpools may turn up some abalone or even a crayfish. Nature is literally at your fingertips in the Bay of Fires.

" We couldn't resist a swim in the crystal-clear waters of the Tasman Sea. We took to the chilly waters with local abalone diver Peter, who braves these temperatures as part of his everyday life! I must say, it took our breath away, but Peter produced the goods, showing off a couple of abalone within 20 minutes.

Our afternoon snorkelling with Peter rolled into a seafood feast down by the St Helens Marina. There were people fishing off the pier and the sun was starting to set, which lit up the yachts on the sparkling water beautifully. To us, this is what is so wonderful about Australia – being surrounded by such raw beauty in the company of welcoming locals. Enjoying freshly caught lobster and some of Tassie's finest wine was also pretty wonderful! "

JEN AND CLINT

PLACES WE GO

The serene natural beauty of the Bay of Fires is incredible. Its clear, crystal-blue water contrasts with the orange/red rocks and white sand, and there's a stillness about the place, despite the crashing waves. It is a place of wonder and awe; more people should know about this Tasmanian secret.

Suzanne Byron, Croydon Hills, Victoria

WHAT TO DO

- Don a wetsuit and dive some of the most diverse temperate-water environments in Australia, exploring kelp forests and searching for the elusive sea dragon.
- Take the four-day guided Bay of Fires Walk, traversing remote and beautiful landscapes and staying in exclusive eco-friendly accommodation.

BICHENO

The 360-degree view from the top of Whalers Lookout near the centre of Bicheno is the perfect introduction to this picturesque Tasmanian seaside town. Turquoise waters meet wide, sandy beaches that resident penguins return to at night. The small township, with its boutique shops and cafes, has everything you need without being overdeveloped. Down on the waterfront, aka 'the Gulch', fisherfolk return each day with their catch, and tourists float over rare marine life and kelp forests in Tasmania's only glass-bottomed boat.

From town, a foreshore track leads to the Blowhole, an incredible natural wonder where the power of the ocean is demonstrated in dramatic saltwater blasts through the boulders. Red-lichen-coated granite rocks are brilliant against the blue sky and ocean.

The area is a magnet for wildlife, with whales, dolphins and sea lions frequently spotted from the coastline. Just out of town, East Coast Natureworld is a sanctuary for Tasmanian devils, kangaroos, wombats and wallabies, and nearby, Douglas-Apsley National Park is home to many rare and endangered species of flora and fauna.

With a chequered history that includes whaling in the early 1800s, Bicheno is primarily a resort town these days, known for its fishing and abundant seafood. With the mildest climate on the state's east coast, it has firmly established itself as a holiday playground.

The drive along the east coast of Tasmania is truly stunning, and one well worth taking. It's dotted with small seaside towns on beautiful white-sand beaches, including the quaint fishing village of Bicheno.

We headed straight to its famous Blowhole, which was certainly putting on a show when we arrived. Water shooting high into the sky was a sight to see and we got quite an unexpected spray! Next we explored the chilly Tasmanian waters in the glass-bottomed boat, which revealed an underwater landscape of rarely seen kelp forests. Within minutes of our journey we were visited by schools of mullet, a small shark and even a seahorse, and we passed sea lions basking in the sun on top of boulders. Our cameraman Gary got to experience things a little closer than we did, braving the 10°C temperatures in a steamer wetsuit to get underwater footage!

We finished with an afternoon at East Coast Natureworld to see endangered Tassie devils. Getting up close to them was a privilege and we were lucky enough to meet 'Monster' and 'Danger', who were nowhere near as scary as their names might suggest. We also got to hand-feed the resident kangaroos, and as we left the Old McDonalds Farm section, our daughter Charli proclaimed: 'This has been the best day ever!'.

JEN AND CLINT

PLACES WE GO

WHAT TO DO

- Visit East Coast Natureworld to get up close to the native wildlife, including Tasmanian devils that are part of a rescue and rehabilitation program.
- Cruise on Tasmania's only glass-bottomed boat and try to spot the elusive weedy sea dragon.
- Join a penguin tour to a local rookery and watch the little penguins return from the sea as the sun sets.
- Scuba dive at one of the best temperate dive locations in the world.

We stood rugged up against the unexpected chill of the late-summer evening, eyes cast upwards to the dimming light of dusk. Then we waited ... At first only a couple arrived, whirring overhead. Then more came – dozens, then hundreds were in sight. The air was soon thick with thousands of shearwaters [a type of long-winged seabird] wheeling overhead, their calls drowning out the rhythmic crash of the waves. Our Bruny Island adventure had only just begun ...

Margaret Seaberg, Caringbah South, New South Wales

» *The lighthouse marking the spectacular and wild coastline*

» *The neck connecting the south and north sections of Bruny Island*

BRUNY ISLAND

» Jen and Clint on an island, which is off an island off an island

An island, off an island (Tasmania), off another island (Australia): just getting to 'Bruny' is an adventure in itself. To get to this wilderness wonderland, head south from Hobart to the town of Kettering, from where you take a 20-minute vehicular ferry across the D'Entrecasteaux Channel. Before you know it, you'll find yourself on an open road, feeling as though you have much of this 100-kilometre-long island to yourself. Indeed, it only has around 600 residents.

The island is actually almost two islands; the north and south sections are connected by a narrow isthmus of land called 'the Neck'. South Bruny National Park is in the southern section, but both ends offer incredible natural beauty. Bushwalk to your heart's content, or forego physical activity and indulge in the plethora of gourmet experiences available, taking advantage of the fresh local seafood, cool-climate grape-growing conditions and great community of passionate artisan producers.

Bruny's adventures continue offshore. Its southern coastline has spectacular sea cliffs, caves and blowholes amid the might of the Southern Ocean, all of which you can take in on a once-in-a-lifetime adventure cruise.

" Bruny Island is an absolute treasure with oodles of natural beauty. It's also home to many passionate artisan producers who have chosen a unique and appealing way of life. As soon as we drove off the ferry, no matter where we went, the locals welcomed us with open arms.

First up we met Nick Haddow from the Bruny Island Cheese Company. Nestled in the bushland, his factory has a small cafe at the front of it, and we could smell freshly ground coffee and homemade cakes as we walked up the path. Inside, the shelves were stacked with homemade cheeses that were simply irresistible.

It was much the same story when we met Joe Bennett from Get Shucked. He is the kind of guy who simply loves his backyard. We tasted oysters fresh out of the water, which was only a hundred metres away. And Joe was shucking them right in front of us – and excitedly told us to add a dash of his mother-in-law's special sauce!

Make sure you've got an appetite when you step onto this island, as you won't be disappointed! "

JEN AND CLINT

PLACES WE GO

» Fresh oysters from Get Shucked

WHAT TO DO

- Observe seal colonies, dolphins, whales and birdlife, as well as the ecological and historical wonder of South Bruny National Park's coastline, on a three-hour adventure with Bruny Island Cruises.
- Take a hike: Bruny Island is a mecca for bushwalkers, offering a range of tracks through the national park or along beaches.
- Climb the steps to Truganini Lookout at 'the Neck' for 360-degree views of the island's north and south sections.
- Head to Bruny Island Cheese Company or Get Shucked to indulge in some of the best cheese and oysters in the country.

CRADLE MOUNTAIN– LAKE ST CLAIR NATIONAL PARK

This was my first helicopter flight and from the moment we departed from close to Cradle Mountain, I was totally in awe of Tasmania's majestic and magical landscape. The mountains and canyons we flew over were magnificent, as were the lakes and walking tracks, where we could even see hikers traversing the rugged terrain. It's a must for every visitor to Tasmania and I would do it again any time.

Brigid Holmes, Yeppoon, Queensland

Conjure up an image of Tasmania and it's likely Cradle Mountain will come to the top of your mind. This iconic mountain, protected within Cradle Mountain–Lake St Clair National Park, is a unique landscape, with its famed craggy peak reaching to the sky and reflective Dove Lake surrounded by pristine forest lying serenely at its feet.

Winter or summer, the park is a playground for adventurers thanks to the world-famous Overland Track, but moreover, its significant wilderness area has earned Cradle Mountain its stripes, gaining it World Heritage status and making it one of Tasmania's most treasured places.

The pristine environment has a diverse plant life and is also home to prolific wildlife, most notably the Tasmanian devil, quolls and platypuses. The national park's heritage is represented by many Aboriginal historic sites, as well as the chalet 'Waldheim'. Waldheim, built in 1912, was the first accommodation for tourists in the park. It was constructed by Gustav and Kate Weindorfer, enthusiastic botanists who believed that the area should be enjoyed by everyone.

Today, the Weindorfers' dream is a reality. Accommodation options abound and the wilderness is accessible to all; you can take the two-hour walk around Dove Lake, the six-day Overland Track hike or even attempt to summit Cradle Mountain.

" Cradle Mountain–Lake St Clair National Park is one of Australia's true wilderness treasures, greatly admired by trekkers right across the world, and especially by us.

As lovers of the outdoors we have spent a lot of time here. All of our trips have varied enormously, and that is part of the appeal. From the six-day Overland Track to a stroll around Dove Lake, no matter where we have explored, we've been overwhelmed by the park's beauty. Surrounded by mountains and ancient rainforests, we always feel a world away from civilisation and replenished by Mother Nature.

We've also enjoyed all forms of accommodation just outside the national park, from the campground where we had wallabies come up to our caravan, to staying at the cosy Cradle Mountain Lodge, where we sat in front of a crackling fire with a red wine in the middle of winter.

Meeting the rangers, we learnt that to work here is a dream come true for many of them – they're here to carry on the legacy of Gustav Weindorfer. "

JEN AND CLINT

PLACES WE GO

WHAT TO DO

- Take any of the beautiful walks in the area, ranging from leisurely to challenging, and appreciate the natural beauty and ancient landscape.
- Stay at Cradle Mountain Lodge, an iconic experience that blends superb accommodation with a true wilderness setting.
- Visit the Devils@Cradle Tasmanian devil sanctuary to see how this threatened species is being supported to ensure its long-term survival.

» Prolific wildlife

» *The famous perspective of Wineglass Bay*

» *Jen and Clint take in the view*

» *Lit up by the sun*

FREYCINET NATIONAL PARK

The landscape of Freycinet is magical and timeless, with smooth rock formations coloured with stunning muted shades of pinks, oranges and blues that sparkle like diamonds when bathed in sunlight. The walk up to the viewing platform overlooking magnificent Wineglass Bay, with its azure water lapping at a perfect horseshoe curve of white sand, leaves you breathless. Your imagination can run wild in this stunning wilderness.

Carol Heys, Margate, Tasmania

» *Kayak around the national park for a different view*

No matter where you look, a picture-postcard scene is before you in this stunning national park. Positioned spectacularly on Tasmania's east coast, the park occupies much of the Freycinet Peninsula and is blessed with natural features including the Hazards – pink and red granite mountains – and Wineglass Bay, voted one of the world's best beaches several times.

The view over Wineglass Bay from the Hazards is almost better than being on the beach itself; the crescent of turquoise water meeting the white sand and granite mountains is instantly recognisable from iconic pictures. And the walking trail to get there, and many other trails, follow in the footsteps of the peninsula's original inhabitants, the Oyster Bay tribe of Tasmanian Aboriginal people.

Beyond Wineglass Bay are the equally stunning Bryans and Cooks Beaches facing Great Oyster Bay, and there is no shortage of secluded coves to escape to. Fishing, snorkelling, rock climbing and taking a scenic cruise are perfect ways to spend your days in Freycinet. And with luxurious lodges and incredible dining in the area, the peninsula fully indulges all the senses.

" When we kayaked on Coles Bay it felt like we were paddling in a postcard; we were treated to the deepest blue sky with the sun lighting up the Hazards. I can't say we paddled much, because we kept on stopping to look up at the granite mountains!

Hiking to the lookout to watch the sun set over Wineglass Bay, we could see why this area has a reputation as one of the most stunning coastlines in Australia. The pristine beaches seem to go on forever. We took it one step further by taking to the skies in a helicopter to get aerial shots for our TV show. It would have to be one of the most incredible places we've filmed, especially as the weather was so good; the water was sparkling, and the Hazards were a beautiful pink.

That night we feasted on Tasmania's spectacular seafood, including fresh lobster and prawns, topped off with a chilled wine. Freycinet really is a beautiful part of the world. "

JEN AND CLINT

PLACES WE GO

WHAT TO DO

- Take a four-wheel-drive trip to the Cape Tourville Lighthouse for incredible outlooks.
- Hike on any number of bushwalking trails for different views of the national park, and meet the resident wildlife along the way.
- Kayak across the turquoise sea for a spectacular view back to land.
- Indulge in local seafood picked straight from one of the world's cleanest oceans.

HOBART

» Boats on Sullivans Cove

Just a quick glance around Hobart, the smallest Australian capital city, tells you of its historical significance. Established in 1804, it was the second city to be formed after Sydney. Today, this former penal colony is full of heritage character and is built around Sullivans Cove, where historic dockside taverns tell the tale of a brisk trade amongst earlier seafarers and traders. It thrived on the whaling and sealing industry and became a city in 1842.

Nestled between Mount Wellington, which dominates the view above the city, and the Derwent Estuary, which surrounds it, Hobart is an undulating streetscape of Georgian buildings filled with world-class arts, culture and food-and-wine establishments. Modern life is bustling on the waterfront, where Salamanca Place hosts the famous Salamanca Market, yet everywhere is relaxed and laid-back, thanks to the city's boutique size and friendly locals.

Put on the world stage most recently thanks to the opening of MONA, the Museum of Old and New Art (see p. 206), Hobart is booming as a cultural mecca. And with its picturesque setting and proximity to some of the state's best attractions, this capital is truly captivating.

" Hobart is one of our favourite places in Tasmania. A bike ride down Mount Wellington gives spectacular views over the water, and is a fun way to get the lay of the land over Tassie's largest city.

The Salamanca Market is a Saturday speciality, with producers from all over the state coming together and supporting each other with their fine food, arts and crafts, and wonderful wines. Tasmania is renowned for its 'paddock to plate' philosophy, and this is highlighted at the market, as everyone celebrates the amazing produce on sale straight from local farms. While we were looking at all the stalls, we kept on bumping into people we'd met on our travels in other parts of the state – it's that kind of community-like place, as is Hobart in general. "

JEN AND CLINT

PLACES WE GO

> Hobart is becoming a cultural heavy weight in Australia, with the subterranean fortress that is MONA and the amazing sights and sounds of the arts and music festival Dark Mofo. While it might seem like an odd contender to be a cosmopolitan capital, it surprises at every turn.
>
> **Amelia Paxman, Bardon, Queensland**

WHAT TO DO

- Stop off at the iconic Saturday market at Salamanca Place for arts, crafts, cuisine and more, all with a local flavour.
- Head up Mount Wellington for an exceptional view over the city and surrounds, and if you are feeling adventurous, join a mountain bike tour back down again.
- Explore the many restaurants and cafes in the city, which all take advantage of Tasmania's outstanding local produce and wine.
- Don't leave without checking out MONA, a privately funded museum housing an incredible collection of old and new art, described as a 'subversive adult Disneyland' by the museum's owner. Check out Moorilla Winery on the same site while you're there.
- Visit Cascade Brewery, Australia's oldest continually operating brewery.

» Cafes lining Salamanca Place

» View from the mountain

» Jen and Clint taking a breather on a bike ride down Mount Wellington

» *The Roaring Forties produces King Island's renowned waves*

KING ISLAND

King Islanders will proudly tell you that they import the world's best surfers and export the world's best produce. This island, between the Victorian and Tasmanian coastlines in the middle of Bass Strait, might be a little remote, but its famous King Island Dairy, stunning beaches and beef and seafood have made sure it's hot on the map of places to go.

King Island's location means that visitors don't have to share its spoils with many other tourists. It also means that you get to know the locals as you make your way around the island's cafes and restaurants, and visit the various producers.

You're sure to be treated to some excellent gourmet experiences in some of the prettiest locations on this island, which seems to revolve around food. Take a hamper packed with local goodies to one of the many scenic picnic spots, such as Disappointment Bay (which, incidentally, does not live up to its name), or pretty Naracoopa Jetty, where you can eat your lunch, or simply catch it.

When you can't possibly fit another oyster or wedge of brie in, take one of the many walking trails around the island to explore the shipwrecks, a big part of King Island's rich maritime history. Finish up in the town of Grassy, waiting for the fairy penguins to make their way home as the sun sets over the Tasman.

» *A jetty sticking out into Bass Strait*

» *King Island's famous cheese*

WHAT TO DO

- Take one of the King Island 'grazing trails' to combine the best of the island's walks with its incredible produce.
- Order a hamper from Foodworks in Currie, the island's largest town, and take it to a scenic location overlooking Bass Strait.
- Visit the cheese-tasting room at King Island Dairy's fromagerie to see where this famous cheese is made.
- Dine at one of the many restaurants for some of the best freshly caught crayfish on the planet.

MONA

The first lesson you'll learn when you enter the Museum of Old and New Art (MONA) in Hobart (*see* p. 202) is to expect the unexpected. The centre of the expansive foyer gives way to a labyrinth of space extending three levels underground, and it is from the very bottom that David Walsh, the man behind this masterpiece, envisioned his visitors would begin their journey.

Forget previously polite experiences at other museums. MONA will dance all over them, kicking up her heels at the end. Walsh wants people to experience his private collection of art without any expectations, with an open mind, and preferably after a stiff drink at the Vault bar, which sits strategically at the point on the lower level where the exhibits begin.

The biggest philanthropic project in Australia for decades, Walsh spent around $80 million building the avant-garde, underground 'Disneyland for adults' to house his private collection, which ranges from the subversive to the disturbing, and largely centres around the themes of sex and death. His intention to 'present art that demands an emotional response' does so without apology, or even much explanation. While visitors get an interactive iPod tracking their journey around the museum, there is little to no information available with each exhibit, so that you are free to interpret them as you wish.

You could sit in front of the theatrically lit exhibits trying to get your head around them for hours, with the sights, sounds and smells almost assaulting you. Love the museum or hate it, the irreverent Walsh will almost certainly achieve his vision of challenging you, and you will burst out of the museum at the end, back into a world of natural light, wondering what exactly happened to you in there.

Arriving by ferry up the Derwent River, MONA appears from its rocky outcrop and fills you with anticipation. You soon realise it is as much a tribute to modern architecture as it is to old and new art. It's best to start your MONA experience at the very bottom of its cavernous depths; for us it was at the bar with a Bloody Mary!

Every room and level delivers something new and challenging. Many of the rooms are simply mesmerising and after 20 minutes you realise you've been staring at one of a hundred freestanding TV screens, watching one of a hundred documentaries in a language you'll never understand!

After a few hours at MONA you burst out into the crisp Tasmanian sunlight and ask: 'When can I do it all again?'

Tammy Walker, Ripponlea, Victoria

DID YOU KNOW?

- Tasmanians gain free entry to MONA. Walsh wanted his fellow compatriots to have easy and regular access to a local gallery that they might otherwise shy away from.
- MONA is built into the cliffs around the Berriedale peninsula on the Derwent River, sharing the land with the award-winning Moorilla winery and craft brewery Moo Brew. Visitors, many of whom arrive by boat from the city, find the winery, cafe, restaurant and accommodation pavilions on the grounds soothing tonics after the palm-sweating experience in the museum.
- You walk over a full-sized tennis court to get to the entrance of the museum, a deliberate contradiction to the grand, imposing entrances most other museums like to create.
- You can shake off the shock with a good bounce on the enormous trampoline in the grounds after your visit.

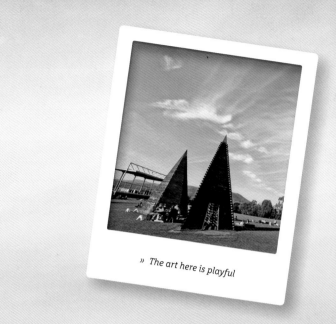

» *The art here is playful*

» *David Walsh's famous fortress of art sits dramatically on the Derwent River*

This place is truly awe-inspiring and filled with history and atmosphere. Just strolling around the grounds evokes an amazing feeling. Walking through the old gaol sends a chill through your body as you think about what must have happened there; the Isle of the Dead is also very moving. We found that everyone walked around quietly, showing a great respect and reverence for Port Arthur. I think this place is somewhere every Australian should visit to better understand colonial Australian history.

Annlea Bruce, Petrie, Queensland

» *The site is mainly well-preserved ruins*

» *Port Arthur is an open-air museum of Tasmania's penal history*

PORT ARTHUR

Australia's most famous convict site, Port Arthur is an intricate and evocative experience, an outdoor museum preserved to enable us to gain an insight into Australia's history and what life was like in one of the most important penal settlements in the 1800s.

Situated on the stunning Tasman Peninsula, the site is home to more than 30 buildings, both ruined and restored, including an imposing penitentiary, dockyards and a hospital. All of the buildings paint a vivid picture of what life was like for some of Britain's most hardened criminals and the guards who worked here.

The non-denominational church, which could accommodate more than 1000 people and was used by the authorities in an attempt to reform through religion, is a testament to the convict builders' skills. Today only the shell remains, its pointed spires reaching to the sky.

Between 1833 and 1877 the population at Port Arthur grew to more than 1100 convicts, some sentenced to hard labour for crimes we would consider petty today. Punishment, both physical and psychological, was routine, and industries such as tree felling and boat building flourished under the labour regime that existed.

Today the beautifully landscaped grounds and gardens are wonderful to stroll around, much like the officers and ladies would have done in the 1800s, shielded from the prisoners' view.

" No matter how many books you read, there's nothing better than being in a place to truly learn about it. And a visit to Port Arthur brings alive the story of the convicts – an important and fascinating chapter in Australia's history.

As soon as we stepped onto the grounds of the old penal colony, which was built by the convicts themselves, we were struck by the haunting energy of the place. With its well-preserved buildings, it's like an open-air museum that gives you great insight into how it would have been for all those who lived here, both the hardened criminals and those who worked here, over 150 years ago.

Our guide Colin had been at Port Arthur for over 20 years, 'longer than most convicts' as he pointed out. He took us for a tour of the main prison, and told stories about the convicts, who did hard labour during the day or were confined to cells that were considered too small even during convict times. Solitary confinement was a punishment you definitely wouldn't want to have experienced ... The prison has long since closed down, but there will always be intrigue about the inmates, and, in fact, about who among us has links to convicts in our families' histories.

While the tour of the whole site was moving, the chapel was the highlight – you could almost hear the ghosts of Port Arthur singing. "

JEN AND CLINT

PLACES WE GO

WHAT TO DO

- Join the nightly ghost tour, exploring the site by lantern light, hearing true and bizarre prisoner stories and braving one of Australia's most apparently haunted locations.

- Take a boat trip to the Isle of the Dead, in the middle of the harbour, where more than 1000 prisoners are buried.

- After an introductory walking tour with one of the Port Arthur guides, take a harbour cruise to view the site from the water and imagine what it must have been like for prisoners to arrive by sea back in the day.

STANLEY

Dominated by 'the Nut', a volcanic plug on the edge of town, Stanley is impossible to miss on a journey to Tasmania's north-west. The Nut rises 152 metres with almost vertical cliffs on three sides plunging into Bass Strait, and at its base is the historic village just begging to be explored.

George Bass and Matthew Flinders discovered the unique formation in 1798, naming it 'Circular Head'; the region's municipality is still called this. It was settled from 1826 after the Van Diemen's Land Company was granted land in the north-west, including the Stanley area, and employees from England arrived in the region. The township was named in 1842 after Lord Stanley – who went on to serve three terms as the British prime minister – and the village eventually became a thriving and bustling centre built around farming.

These days, tourism and fishing are its major drawcards, with people flocking to see the incredible views both of and from the Nut. Surrounded by beautiful coastline, and with heritage buildings and terraced streets, this 'edge of the world' town with its mix of natural and historical wonder is certainly worth a visit.

" You can see why Stanley is often referred to as 'the edge of the world', perched as it is next to the Nut, a little piece of land that drops off into Bass Strait.

Our first port of call, like most travellers I would say, was a chairlift ride to the top of the Nut. We were lucky enough to be joined by a fifth-generation local man, Graham, who runs a B&B in town. To meet someone with such a long family history in Australia is quite rare, but it's a common occurrence in Stanley. Home to some of the freshest air in the world, the breeze from the top of the Nut certainly blows out any cobwebs, and the views of the beaches on all sides are breathtaking.

The town itself is charming, with its lovingly restored buildings that house cafes, art and craft shops, and B&Bs. Many of the original English settler buildings have been preserved, and a drive around town is fascinating. There's Highfield, a historic house built in 1841 that's regarded as the birthplace of the European settlement of Tasmania's north-west, and you can even see the former home of Joseph Lyons, Australia's tenth prime minister who took office in 1923.

But it's not just the town and the Nut that are beautiful. We took a scenic helicopter flight out to the nearby Tarkine wilderness area, a huge expanse of cool temperate rainforest that contains Aboriginal archaeological sites – it really is a stunning place. "

JEN AND CLINT

PLACES WE GO

This beautiful historical fishing village is a place everyone should see. A lazy little town set under the Nut, this place has so much history, it will take you back to the early settler days. Gorgeous beaches to boot, and lots of restaurants to tickle your tastebuds.

Jenny Barnes, Launceston, Tasmania

WHAT TO DO

- Climb the Nut, or if the challenge is too great, take the chairlift for incredible views over the north-west coastline and Stanley.

- Explore the historical township, which has a number of heritage buildings that have not changed over the years, including the Van Diemen's Land Company store.

- Join a penguin tour or hop aboard a seal cruise to encounter some of the region's local residents.

» Stanley's iconic Nut

» *The historic outpost on the edge of the Tasmanian Wilderness.*

STRAHAN

On the wonderful wild-west coast of Tasmania, Strahan is blessed with rugged beauty, quaint old houses, the magnificent Gordon River, wilderness and quiet isolation. Get lost in the peace and serenity and rejuvenate your soul. It's magic.

Clare Taylor, Toongabbie, New South Wales

On the doorstep of Tasmanian World Heritage wilderness in the state's south-west, the harbour-side village of Strahan is full of stories about Indigenous inhabitants, convicts, pioneers, miners, piners and environmental warriors. Aboriginal occupation in the area can be traced back at least 35,000 years, with archaeological finds that are among the earliest evidence of human habitation anywhere in the world.

Originally established by Europeans as a port for the copper-mining settlements in the region, it also became an important hub for the timber industry that surrounded Macquarie Harbour (around which the town is based), which focused on the fabled and sought-after Huon pine. The town was known as Long Bay or Regatta Point until the late 1800s, when it was formally named Strahan after a governor of the time.

The narrow mouth of Macquarie Harbour was nicknamed 'Hell's Gates' by convicts destined for the penal colony on nearby Sarah Island; the convicts claimed that the shallow and quite dangerous opening was their entrance to hell. Macquarie Harbour Penal Station on the island, which operated between 1822 and 1833, had the reputation of being one of the cruellest penal settlements in the colonies.

Today Strahan has a population of only around 630, but it is a bustling, boutique tourist town famous for the nearby World Heritage wilderness, which can be found on wild and remote waters in the neighbouring Franklin-Gordon Wild Rivers National Park. The largest expanse of temperate rainforest in the world, this is a land of cascading waterfalls, wild mountains and dramatic gorges, and was the scene for one of the most epic conservation battles in Australia: the fight to save the Gordon and Franklin Rivers from a proposed hydro-electric dam.

" We still have a Huon pine wooden boat that we bought in Strahan on our mantelpiece – this harbour-side town made quite the impression on us. The scenic boat ride on the Gordon River was beautiful; we were surrounded by World Heritage wilderness – and it really is *wild*. We all commented on how ethereal the place felt, especially as we got further away from the town – the rich Aboriginal history in this part of the world certainly contributed to that feeling.

Locals on board the boat recounted stories of the region, showed us old bluestone buildings built by convicts, and shared how they passionately fought against the damming of the Gordon River, in one of the most significant environmental campaigns in Australia's history.

After strolling the 19th-century streets of the quaint town, we visited an old sawmill and watched how salvaged pieces of Huon pine, taken from the forest floor, were delicately sculpted into all sorts of objects, including dinner plates, bowls and the boat we still treasure today. "

JEN AND CLINT

PLACES WE GO

WHAT TO DO

- Join a Gordon River Cruise to explore the World Heritage wilderness, crossing the harbour, gliding through world-class rainforest and visiting the ruins of Sarah Island.

- Take the short drive out to Ocean Beach, Tasmania's longest beach. Set on the wild Southern Ocean, you can feel the 'roaring forties' hit your face, all the way from Antarctica or South America.

- Wander Strahan's 19th-century streets and enjoy fine food and wine.

INDEX

PHOTO CREDITS

Front cover
Diving in the Great Barrier Reef near Port Douglas, Queensland (Ross Isaacs/Ocean Planet Images/Tourism Australia)

Back cover
The wide, open road near Alice Springs, Northern Territory (Courtesy of *Places We Go*)

Back endpaper
Marine life in the Great Barrier Reef, Queensland (Pinosub/Shutterstock.com)

Title pages
In front of Maguk Gorge, Kakadu National Park, Northern Territory (Courtesy of *Places We Go*)

Introduction
Sand dunes in Fraser Island, Queensland (Courtesy of *Places We Go*)

NEW SOUTH WALES & ACT
Pages x–1 PWG; 2 Geoff Lung/TA; 3 Selfiy/Shutterstock.com; 4 James Horan/DNSW; 5 Vance Parker/Shutterstock.com; 6 (a) Brian Geach/TA (b) Andrew Wallace/TA (c) Yusuke Ishibashi/TA; 9 (a) Jeff Drewitz/TA (b) PWG (c) Mike Newling/TA; 10 (a) Coffs Coast Marketing/DNSW (b) Cameron Ernst/Virgin Australia (c) Ian Spagnolo/DNSW; 11 Coffs Coast Marketing/DNSW; 13 PWG; 14 (a) & (b) PWG (c) Murray Vanderveer/DNSW; 16 (a) Rory McGuinness/TA (b) Capella Lodge; 17 Capella Lodge; 18 Don Fuchs/DNSW; 19 (a) Roberto Seba (b) PWG; 20 North Sullivan/DNSW; 21 (a) Nick Rains/DNSW (b) North Sullivan/DNSW; 22 DNSW; 23 (a) Sorrel Wilby/TA (b) Andrew Brown/DNSW; 24 James Horan/DNSW; 25 Brett Parkes/TA; 26 Ethan Rohloff/DNSW; 27 (a) Tiffany Cherry (b) Masaru Kitano/TA; 29 (a) Murray Vanderveer/DNSW (b) Tamworth Country Music Festival/Tourism Tamworth; 30 PWG

VICTORIA
32–33 PWG; 34 TV; 35 Peter Dunphy/Daylesford and Macedon Ranges; 36 (a) TV (b) & (c) Mark Watson Incite Images/TV; 37 PWG; 38 (a) TV (b) PWG; 41 (a) TV (b) PWG (c) Kristoffer Paulsen/TA; 42–45 PWG; 46 TV; 47 AFL Media; 49 Peter Dunphy/TV; 50 PWG; 53 (a) Peter Dunphy/TV (b) Adrian Brown/TA (c) David Mitchener/TV; 54–55 PWG; 57 (a) TV (b) PWG (c) TV (d) PWG; 58 (a) TV (b) & (c) PWG (d) TV; 61 (a) TV (b) & (c) PWG; 62 PWG; 65 (a) & (b) Adrian Brown/TA (c) Bikeriderlondon/Shutterstock.com

SOUTH AUSTRALIA
66–67 PWG; 68 (a) Kelvin Wong/Shutterstock.com (b) Brett Sheriden/SATC (c) PWG; 71 (a) Sven Kovac/SATC (b) Brett Sheridan/SATC (c) Adam Bruzzone/TA; 72 (a) Adam Bruzzone/SATC (b) Mike Annese/SATC (c) Lachlan Swan; 74 PWG; 75 (a) Greg Snell/South Australian Wildlife Caretaker (b) Neale Winter/SATC (c) PWG; 76 (a) Neale Winter/SATC (b) Greg Snell/TA; 77 Greg Snell/TA; 79 (a) D'Arnberg Wines (b) Adrian Brown/TA; 80 (a) Kerry Lorrimer/Wild Bush Luxury (b) Adam Bruzzone/SATC (c) PWG; 83 (a) Adam Bruzzone/TA (b) & (c) PWG; 84 Greg Snell/South Australia Wildlife Caretaker; 85 (a) PWG (b) Greg Snell/South Australia Wildlife Caretaker; 87 (a) Alex Makeyev/SATC (b) Adam Bruzzone/SATC; 88 PWG; 90–91 Adam Bruzzone/SATC

WESTERN AUSTRALIA
92–96 PWG; 97 (a) Evan Collis/TWA (b) TWA; 98 TA; 99 PWG; 100 TWA; 101 Nick Rains/TA; 102 (a) TWA (b) PWG; 103 PWG; 105 (a) PWG (b) & (c) TWA; 106 (a) & (b) PWG (c) TWA; 108 PWG; 109 (a) PWG (b) Evan Collis/TWA; 110 PWG; 113 (a) PWG (b) TWA (c) PWG; 114 PWG; 117 (a) Janelle Lugge/Shutterstock.com (b) & (c) PWG; 118–119 PWG; 120 (a) TWA (b) PWG; 121–125 TWA; 126 Ian Lever/TA; 127 PWG; 128 Australia's Coral Coast/TWA; 129 (a) TWA (b) Richard Gale/Australia's Coral Coast

NORTHERN TERRITORY
130–132 PWG; 134 Adrian Brown/TA; 135 PWG; 136 (a) Great Southern Rail (b) TA (c) PWG; 139 (a) Steve Strike/TNT (b) PWG; 140 (a) Peter Eve/TNT (b) PWG; 141 PWG; 143 (a) TA (b) PWG; 144 Steve Strike/TNT (b) PWG; 145 PWG; 146 TNT; 147 (a) TA (b) PWG; 148–155 PWG; 156 Robert Wallace/TA

QUEENSLAND
158–159 PWG; 160 (a) PWG (b) Adam Bruzzone TA (c) PWG; 162 (a) Tourism and Events Queensland (b) Jon Armstrong/TA; 163 Tourism and Events Queensland; 164 (a) PWG (b) Maxime Coquard/TA; 166 Tourism and Events Queensland; 167 Tourism and Events Queensland; 168 (a) Masaru Kitano/TA (b) Susan Wright/TA; 171 (a) PWG (b) Maxime Coquard/TA (c) Marco Saracco/Shutterstock.com; 172 (a) Stephen Nutt/TA (b) Darren Jew/TA (c) PWG; 175 PWG; 176 (a) PWG (b) Maxime Coquard/TA; 179 (a) Thala Beach Lodge (b) Ross Isaacs/TA; 180 Maxime Coquard/TA; 181 Maxime Coquard/TA; 183 (a) John Montesi/TA (b) Tourism and Events Queensland; 184 (a) Tourism and Events Queensland (b) PWG; 187 (a) Maxime Coquard/TA (b) PWG; 188 PWG

TASMANIA
190–191 PWG; 192 (a) & (b) PWG (c) Glenn Gibson/TT; 193 Glenn Gibson/TT; 195 PWG; 196 Rob Burnett/TT; 197 (a) Rob Burnett/TT (b) PWG; 199 PWG; 200 (a) Rob Burnett/TT (b) PWG (c) Andrew Mcintosh Ocean Photography/TT; 201 Rob Burnett/TT; 202 Ellenor Argyropoulos/TA; 203 (a) PWG (b) Joe Shemesh/TA (c) Ellenor Argyropoulos/TA; 204 Stuart Owen Fox/TA; 205 (a) Graham Freeman/TA (b) Nick Osborne/TT; 207 (a) Leigh Carmichael (b) Graham Freeman/TA; 208 (a) Jonathan Wherrett/Port Arthur Historic Site Management (b) TA; 211 (a) Graham Freeman/TA (b) PWG; 212 Dan Fellow/TT

ABBREVIATIONS
DNSW Destination New South Wales
PWG *Places We Go*
SATC South Australian Tourism Commission
TA Tourism Australia
TNT Tourism NT
TT Tourism Tasmania
TV Tourism Victoria
TWA Tourism Western Australia

About *Places We Go*

Places We Go is a much-loved international TV travel series that airs right across Australia on Networks Ten and One, and throughout Asia, Europe and the Middle East. It's all about inspiring people through the world to travel in a refreshingly real and authentic way. The show was a dream for former newsreader Jennifer Adams who had spent her life hoping that one day she could share what she'd experienced and learnt on her travels with friends and family.

The TV series came to life with a small but incredibly talented team of people who shared a passion for travel. In those early days, the *Places We Go* edit suite was in a spare room and the voice-over booth in a broom cupboard! But that didn't stop the show's first series being broadcast on both Network Ten and the Discovery Channel throughout South-East Asia and the Pacific Rim and being enjoyed by millions of people. At that time, Jennifer's partner Clint Bizzell was an AFL footballer, and he would join filming expeditions when he could. As soon as he retired from AFL football he too hit the road as co-host.

After two series of international destinations for *Places We Go*, Jennifer and Clint embarked on an adventure of a lifetime – a four-and-a-half-month road trip around Australia, filming the popular 13-part TV travel series *The Great Aussie Drive* under the banner of *Places We Go*. With both their mothers, their then two-year-old daughter, a cameraman and a couple of adventurous friends, they literally drove to every corner of the continent, and were welcomed in by heartwarming locals who wanted to share their spectacular backyards.

Since that trip five years ago, Jennifer and Clint continue to travel extensively throughout Australia, sharing their adventures on TV and inspiring thousands of others to also hit the road and explore our spectacular country.

The essence of *Places We Go* will always remain the same: it's all about real people who simply love to travel.

Jennifer Adams
Founder, Host and Producer/Writer

Places We Go is Jennifer's dream come true. As a founder of the TV series, she's been to some of the most stunning places on the planet and met so many amazing people. Jennifer's been carving out a career in media for over 20 years, from news reporter, to newsreader, documentary filmmaker and traveller. Through her production company Eve Media, she has turned her wish of 'bringing the world a little closer' into a reality with *Places We Go*.

Whether it's climbing a mountain, swimming alongside whale sharks or going on a driving adventure with her partner Clint and their six-year-old daughter Charli, Jennifer redefines the word 'adventure' and takes all of us along for the ride!

Clint Bizzell
Host and Producer

With a love of travel, film and sharing good times with friends, Clint has enjoyed many adventures on the *Places We Go* journey. From climbing mountains to finding himself in bronco-branding competitions in the outback, Clint is always up for a good time with great people and willing to give anything a go – always with a smile on his face! In Clint's life before the TV show, he enjoyed 12 years as an AFL footballer – playing for both Geelong and Melbourne. It's the same passion and love of a team environment that he brings to the *Places We Go* family – he always loves to bring people together on a journey, including the viewer!

AUTHORS' ACKNOWLEDGEMENTS

We would like to acknowledge and thank our incredible *Places We Go* team, which has supported us both on the road and behind the scenes, and contributed to making this book possible.

Special thanks to the amazing Emma De Fry for your tireless work and passion, not only as a fundamental member of the team as a producer and marketing guru, but also for helping us write *Australia's Top 100 Places to Go*. You inspire us daily with your love for travel and humanity.

To our wonderful cameramen: thank you for the amazing sunrises and sunsets! Thanks also to our musical director Tai, who has been on this journey from day one, and to our audio engineer Ian, who always keeps us in check! To our fellow *Places We Go* hosts Caroline, Jesse and Darren, thanks for always being up for a challenge, and thanks to Sharon for helping us canvas the Australian public through the competition for this book.

A big thank you to the very talented *Places We Go* editor Kevin Manning for your passion and integrity in telling great stories, and thank you to our wonderful commercial manager Chris Giannopoulos, who helps us deliver the show around the world and assisted in bringing this book to life.

To our families: thank you for your unwavering support, without which none of this would have been possible. A special thanks to our mothers Eileen and Carol for not only helping us with our daughter on the road (in some very remote and amazing places!), but for being integral members of the crew, always bringing your adventurous spirits and sense of humour.

Thank you to our amazing daughter Charli Grace who has been on the road with us since she was three months old. No adventure could ever be as great as the one we share with you. What a delight you are.

Thank you to Melissa Kayser and Astrid Browne at Hardie Grant Explore for your guidance and for being so excited about the project. Thank you also to Erika Budiman for your beautiful design, and to our editor Michelle Bennett for not only questioning the smallest detail, but for also being inspired by the amazing destinations in this book.

Jen and Clint x

Acknowledgements

The publisher would like to acknowledge the following individuals and organisations:

Editorial manager
Melissa Kayser

Editor
Michelle Bennett

Editorial assistance
Alison Proietto, Lauren Whybrow

Contributing writer
Emma De Fry

Cartography
Bruce McGurty, Emily Maffei

Design
Erika Budiman

Layout
Megan Ellis

Index
Max McMaster

Pre-press
Splitting Image; Megan Ellis

Explore Australia Publishing Pty Ltd
Ground Floor, Building 1, 658 Church Street,
Richmond, VIC 3121

Explore Australia Publishing Pty Ltd is a division of
Hardie Grant Publishing Pty Ltd

Published by Explore Australia Publishing Pty Ltd, 2014

Concept, maps, form and design © Explore Australia
Publishing Pty Ltd, 2014
Text © Jennifer Adams & Clint Bizzell from *Places We Go*, 2014

A Cataloguing-in-Publication entry is available from the
catalogue of the National Library of Australia at www.nla.gov.au

The maps in this publication incorporate data
© Commonwealth of Australia (Geoscience Australia), 2006.
Geoscience Australia has not evaluated the data as altered
and incorporated within this publication, and therefore gives
no warranty regarding accuracy, completeness, currency or
suitability for any particular purpose.

ISBN-13 9781741174601

10 9 8 7 6 5 4 3 2 1

Printed and bound in China by 1010 Printing International Ltd

Publisher's note: Every effort has been made to ensure
that the information in this book is accurate at the time
of going to press. The publisher welcomes information
and suggestions for correction or improvement.
Email: info@exploreaustralia.net.au

Publisher's disclaimer: The publisher cannot accept
responsibility for any errors or omissions. The representation
on the maps of any road or track is not necessarily evidence of
public right of way. The publisher cannot be held responsible
for any injury, loss or damage incurred during travel. It is vital
to research any proposed trip thoroughly and seek the advice
of relevant state and travel organisations before you leave.

www.exploreaustralia.net.au
Follow us on Twitter: @ExploreAus
Find us on Facebook: www.facebook.com/exploreaustralia